Before Rocket

The steam locomotive up to 1829

Anthony Dawson

ACKNOWLEDGEMENTS

In writing this book I would like to thank Andy Mason for his continued support of my writing endeavours and for his accompanying me on various research expeditions. I should also like to thank Andy Guy, co-ordinator of the Early Railways Group of the Railway & Canal Historical Society for peer review of this text, and for his clarifications. So too Sheila Middleton, archivist of the Middleton Railway Trust. Thanks too to the support and friendship of the Railway Volunteers at the Science & Industry Museum, Manchester and the National Railway Museum, York.

Unless stated otherwise, all the images are by the author or from his collection.

First published in Great Britain in 2020
by Gresley Books
an imprint of Mortons Books Ltd.
Media Centre
Morton Way
Horncastle LN9 6JR
www.mortonsbooks.co.uk

ISBN 978 1 911658 25 2

Typeset by ATG Media
Printed and bound in Great Britain

10 9 8 7 6 5 4 3 2 1

Contents

Why replace the horse?

The Rainhill Trials of October 1829 were the coming of age of the railway locomotive. Before a concourse of an estimated 10,000 spectators, the locomotive demonstrated its superiority over using horses, or rope-haulage via stationary engine.

But the locomotive was not new: it was a quarter of a century old. This book charts the development of the locomotive up to the delivery of *Rocket* by Robert Stephenson & Co of Newcastle in September 1829; charting how it evolved from the lumbering curiosities of Richard Trevithick's first pioneering attempts to a machine which could be found at work across the north of England and also in Europe.

But why replace the horse? Between 1792 and 1815 Britain was almost constantly at war with Republican France; a war which was not necessarily popular and one which drove up the cost of living for many.

It was also the start of the industrial revolution with the mechanisation of, in particular, the cloth industry. Employers were looking toward machines to increase productivity and reduce costs. The steam engine – as developed by Matthew Boulton and James Watt – had driven this transformation, and a transport revolution was taking place with the construction of canals and new turnpike roads. The prime mover on roads, canal and industry (including colliery waggonways) was the horse, but the Napoleonic wars had led to the cost of horses nearly doubling due to demand from the military.

Furthermore, the cost of their fodder was steadily rising, with prices for horses and corn reaching an all-time high between 1812 and 1814. This was in part due to bad harvests, but also demand from the military to feed the army.

Furthermore, as part of the war effort against France, there was also a heavy tax on horses. Thus the introduction of locomotives reduced the reliance upon horses (and expenses associated with them); reduced the number of employees and thus labour costs; and reduced transportation costs because a single locomotive (despite its high initial cost) could move a greater load than a horse, required fewer employees to manage it and could burn cheap coal from the mine rather than expensive corn and hay a horse required.

It is not surprising that colliery owners and managers such as John Blenkinsop in Leeds, Christopher Blackett at Wylam or the Grand Allies at Killingworth all began their locomotive projects around 1811-1812 when the cost of horses, food and labour were at their highest.[1] The prices of horses dropped dramatically with cessation of hostilities due to reduced demand, but primarily from the market being flooded with former army horses sold at 'rock bottom' prices.

The reduction in the cost of horses from circa 1815 to circa 1824 resulted in many giving up experiments with the locomotive, but the likes of George Stephenson, William Chapman and John Buddle thought they were worth persevering with. There was another spike in the cost of horses from 1824-1825, and again 1827-1828 which inspired further phases of locomotive building.[2]

Chapter 1
Richard Trevithick
1802-1814

Richard Trevithick (1771-1833), the 'Cornish Giant', is generally considered to have built the first steam locomotive. Trevithick had been a pioneer of using 'strong steam' usually around 50psi, compared to the low pressure condensing engines of Boulton and Watt. By using high pressure steam, Trevithick was able to develop a compact yet powerful steam plant suitable for a variety of tasks.

He was also quick to appreciate that a high pressure engine, if built sufficiently lightly, could become self-moving. He built his first

ABOVE: Richard Trevithick, the 'father' of high-pressure steam and the railway locomotive.

road carriage in 1801 and his London steam coach in 1803, but while they did work, they were impractical due to the poor state of the roads.

Thus, it was natural that he would then turn his attention to a self-moving steam engine on rails. The number of locomotives actually built by Trevithick is disputed, and as Jim Rees and Andy Guy argued in 2003, whether they were intended to be locomotives per-se or something more akin to a 'steam Swiss army knife', a self-moving steam engine capable of a hauling loads but also being able to to run stationary machinery, is open to debate.[3] Rees and Guy posited a list of five locomotives which were definitely by Trevithick (Penydarren; Gateshead; Catch Me Who Can; West India Docks; Plymouth Breakwater) and five potential or 'derived' Trevithick designs which include the Coalbrookdale locomotive, reputed to be the world's first steam locomotive.[4]

COALBROOKDALE 1802

Trevithick's first locomotive is generally considered to have been built in 1802 for the Coalbrookdale Company, owned by the Quaker ironmaster William Reynolds. The problem is, Trevithick's own statement of August 1802 merely refers to 'a carriage... for the real-roads'. There is evidence that castings were made for a steam engine and that Trevithick was paid for testing a pumping engine, but that doesn't necessarily

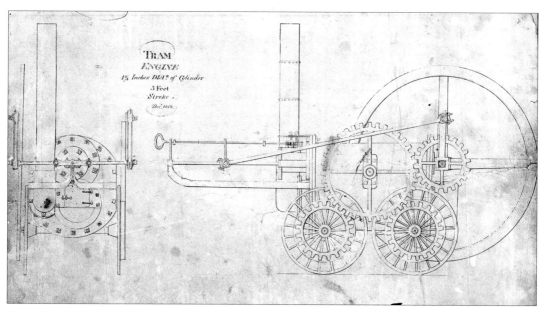

ABOVE: Trevithick 'Tram Engine' drawing of December 1803: once believed to depict the Penydarren locomotive, further study suggested a gauge of only 3ft, with suggestions that it represented the tentative Coalbrookdale Locomotive or an as yet unknown locomotive in South Wales. *(Science & Society Picture Library)*

mean that it was a locomotive. Being so far removed in time, it is not possible to confirm it was ever completed.[5] Thus as Rees and Guy concluded: 'It may not have been steam, may not have been a locomotive and may not have been a Trevithick engine', noting that Matthew Murray of Leeds (Chapter 2) has also designed and patented a portable high pressure steam engine at the same time.[6]

Recent research throws new light on the situation. The enigmatic 'Tram Engine' drawing dated December 1803, which has traditionally been thought to represent the Penydarren Engine (despite incompatibility of dimensions) and later, because of its 3ft gauge, to show the Coalbrookdale engine, instead may represent a hitherto unknown Trevithick locomotive.

The Tram Engine drawing was found in South Wales in 1855, and oral tradition suggested that the engine had in fact been built and used on the 'old navigation tramway' 'about the same time Trevithick

was at Merthyr'.[7] In 2019 a radical new interpretation for the Tram Engine drawing was presented, that it possibly represents a 'lost' Trevithick engine built for the Tredegar Iron Works in South Wales, which may have run on the 3ft gauge Sirhowy Tramway, part of Samuel Homfray's business empire, which also included the Penydarren Iron Works. Thus, it is possible that 'Homfray, enthused by Trevithick's progress… persuaded him to design a similar but smaller version for Tredegar'.[8] Indeed Trevithick notes that his Penydarren locomotive was too big for the job, and intended building a smaller, lighter one, but this was probably for Homfray at Penydarren rather than elsewhere.

PENYDARREN, 1804

Trevithick's most well-known locomotive was that which he built for the Penydarren Iron works in 1804. And, as noted earlier, despite the appearance of the engine being supposedly well-known, the 1803 drawing which is traditionally said to represent the engine does not.

Furthermore, given the very limited clearances of the Plymouth Tunnel on the Penydarren tramroad, a large flywheel and tall chimney simply would not fit, ruling out the Tram Engine and the 'Gateshead' engine designs.

The Tram Engine drawing has the cylinder and cross-head arrangement at the same end as the chimney. This is a very impractical layout making tending the fire and checking water levels only possible when the locomotive was stationary, and is perhaps better suited to a stationary engine which was used intermittently and which could be tended to while not in motion. Given that Trevithick said the Penydarren engine was very manageable, and that Davies Giddy notes it was built to be convenient for the driver to work the engine and for the

ABOVE: A working replica of the 'Tram Engine' was built at Ironbridge Museum in 1990, purporting to represent the 'carriage… for the real roads' mentioned by Trevithick in August 1802. The replica is occasionally steamed at Blists Hill Victorian Town, part of the Ironbridge Gorge Museum. *(Matthew Riccheza)*

ABOVE: The precise form of the 1804 Penydarren locomotive is unknown, but it was probably similar to the 1805 Gateshead locomotive. This working replica was built in 1981 by the Welsh Industrial and Maritime Museum in Cardiff with help of NCB apprentices. It is now on display at the National Waterfront Museum, Swansea.

witnesses to see what was going on, this would probably rule out the cylinder being at the same end as the chimney. Thus, it is more likely that the Penydarren locomotive had the cylinder at the opposite end to the chimney and firebox, somewhat analogous with the Gateshead Engine (opposite below) which is the subject of a replica at the National Waterfront Museum in Swansea.[9]

What is known about the Penydarren engine is that it had four wheels; a cast iron boiler containing a wrought-iron flue; a rolled iron chimney; and a single cylinder 8½ inches bore by 4ft 6in stroke and that it weighed about five tons without water in the boiler. Its actual configuration is unknown, but Guy et al have presented a tentative reconstruction of the engine based on known dimensions and Trevithick practice.[10]

One of the most important observations about the Penydarren locomotive is regarding the effect of exhaust steam in the chimney on the fire. Despite a lengthy and often acrimonious debate in the pages of the technical and domestic press during 1857-1858 – dubbed the 'Battle of the Blastpipe' – it is evident that Richard Trevithick first observed and understood the principal of the blast pipe on his 1804 locomotive: 'The fire burns much better when the steam goes up the chimney then when the engine is idle', and later reinforced the point 'it makes the draught much stronger by going up the chimney'. This was an observation shared by others, including Davies Giddy who remarked:

Everyone looked as attentively as possible into the fire-place; while the engine moved at the rate of a few strokes a minute; and all agreed in declaring, that the fire brightened each time the steam obtained admission into the chimney, as the engine made its stroke.[11]

It is also worth noting that Trevithick also discharged the exhaust steam from the cylinder of his stationary engines into the chimney as well. They became known as 'puffers' from the distinctive sound they made from the exhaust steam in the chimney. As E L Ahrons put it in 1927: 'The effect [of the blast pipe] was there in nature and quality.'[12]

Trevithick's other breakthrough was that of adhesion. Major Nicholas-Joseph Cugnot's (1725-1804) steam carriage of 1770 had shown the viability of an adhesion-worked steam vehicle, albeit on the road rather than rail. Not only did Trevithick observe that a smooth wheel on an iron rail had sufficient adhesion to propel the engine (and a useful load) he tested it also:

There is no doubt about the wheels turning round as you suppose, for when that engine in Wales travelled on the tramroad, which was very smooth, yet all the power could not slip round the wheels when the engine was chained to the post for that particular experiment.[13]

As with understanding the role of exhaust steam in the chimney, claims have been made that Trevithick did not comprehend adhesion, particularly because his 1802 patent states 'we do occasionally, or in certain cases, make the external periphery of the wheels uneven' to help the wheels grip. The operative word is 'occasionally', but there is no evidence this was ever utilised. Despite this, supporters of William Hedley (Chapter 4) claim *he* was the progenitor of the adhesion-worked locomotive, even though Hedley's patent (1813) made a similar claim as Trevithick about making his wheels rough for the purpose of adhesion – and using a rack and pinion (like Blenkinsop (Chapter 2)) or even a chain (*à la* Chapman and Buddle (Chapter 3)) to impel the locomotive forward, particularly on gradients.[14] Although he never built such an engine, Trevithick also deserves the credit for the use of two cylinders working cranks set 90° apart, by which means the action of the engine became more 'equable' and 'it [became] unnecessary to load the work with a fly[wheel].' This was another crucial breakthrough in the development of the locomotive.

CRAWSHAY'S WAGER

The Penydarren engine was famously the subject of a 500 guinea wager between Samuel Homfray and Richard Crawshay as to whether it could take a load of ten tons down the full length of the line, accompanied by only a single man, and then return with the empties. The trip to decide the bet was made on February 21, 1804. Trevithick wrote the next day:

Yesterday we proceeded on our journey with the engine; we carry'd ten tons of Iron, five waggons, and 70 Men riding on them the whole of the journey. Its above 9 miles which we perform'd in 4 hours & 5 mints, but we had to cut down som trees and remove some Large rocks out of the road. The engine, while working, went nearly 5miles pr hour, there was no water put into the boiler from the time we started untill we arriv'd at our journey's end. The coal consumed was 2Hund'd [weight]. On our return home abt 4 miles from the shipping place of the iron, one of the small bolts that fastened the axel to the boiler broak, and let all the water out of the boiler, which prevented the engine returning untill this evening.[15]

The *Cambrian* newspaper (February 24, 1804) confirmed the trip had taken place and added that 'it is not doubted but that the number of horses in the kingdom will be very considerably reduced, and the machine, in the hands of the present proprietors, will be made use of in a thousand instances never yet thought of for an engine.'

Anthony Hill, who acted as judge, proved to be a hair-splitter and refused to pay the bet on the basis of several quibbles, including the track being slewed through the Plymouth Tunnel and the failure of the water pump.[16]

The Penydarren engine had clearly been built to be a railway locomotive and in its design Trevithick intended to make it as light as practicable. It was also far more than a machine built to win a bet. It was 'much more manageable than horses' and was easily able to draw a load of 10 tons. In his letters to Giddy, Trevithick notes it was at work for several days, running the full 9½ miles of the Penydarren tramway. Trevithick also planned that the engine should pull Homfray's coach:

'We… intend to take out the horses of the coach and fasten it to the engine and draw them home.' The locomotive was also clearly intended to be able to demonstrate the utility of high-pressure steam being used to pump water, 'then go by itself from the pump and work a hammer, and then to wind coal, and lastly go to the journey on the road with iron'. Sadly, the engine was found to be too heavy for the brittle cast-iron plateway, a problem which would dog many early locomotive designers until durable wrought-iron rails had been developed. Latterly the Penydarren engine spent its days working a trip hammer before finding its way to the Ffos y Fran pit as a winding engine, where it was probably scrapped in 1859.[17]

Sadly, further development at Penydarren came to naught due to the prickly Trevithick falling out with Homfray, who subsequently purchased the patent rights to produce high pressure engines – including locomotives – and thus Trevithick was no longer entitled to build or erect those engines. Thus when Christopher Blackett, the owner of Wylam (Chapter 4), approached Trevithick circa 1809 to build him a locomotive Trevithick informed him he had 'nothing more to do with the engine business'.[18]

GATESHEAD LOCOMOTIVE (1805)

Trevithick's Gateshead locomotive is known only from drawings; as Rees & Guy (2003) have stated, the position of the Gateshead locomotive is the reverse of that of Penydarren – its physical form is known but little of its history. It is probable that the locomotive was built by John Whinfield – Trevithick's agent in the North East – with the assistance of Trevithick's foreman, John Steele. It was probably built speculatively, perhaps for the Wylam Waggonway, but was too heavy for

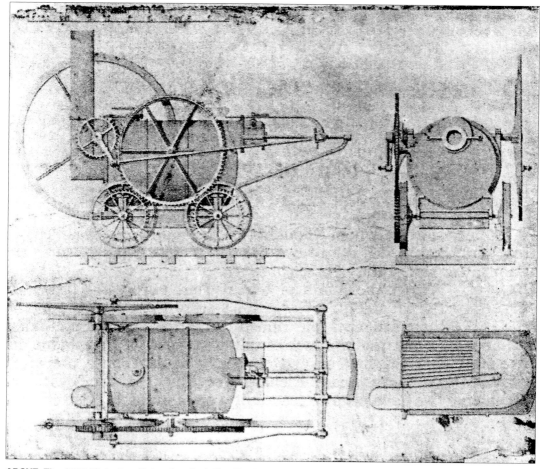

ABOVE: The 1805 'Gateshead' drawing depicting Trevithick's third locomotive built by John Whinfield and his foreman John Steel. *(After Warren 1923)*

the wooden rails then in use.[19] That said, the engineer Robert Wilson of Gateshead (Chapter 7) noted in May 1805 that:

I saw an engine this day upon a new plan it is to draw three waggons of coals up on the Wylam waggon-way... the Engine is to travile with the waggons each waggon with the coals weighs about three-and-half tons and the Engine weighs four-and-a-half tons the Engine is to work without vacuum [i.e. high pressure rather than condensing].

He goes on to say the cylinder was seven inches bore, 3ft stroke and 'placed inside the Boilar and the fire is inside also'. The expected rate of travel was 4mph.[20] Reputedly

it was taken off its wheels and used for the next 60 years working in an iron foundry.[21]

CATCH ME WHO CAN (1808)

All of Trevithick's locomotives are enigmatic, none more so that *Catch Me Who Can*, built in 1808, and again the subject of a wager.

Traditionally said to have been built by John Hazledine and John Rastrick, recent research suggests it may have been built, or at least assembled, by William Rowley, engine builder of London, using a borrowed stationary engine from work on the Thames Archway.[22] *Catch Me Who Can* was based on the standard Trevithick high-pressure 'power unit' consisting of a cast-iron boiler with return-flue with a vertical cylinder immersed in the rear of the boiler an example of which (No. 14) was rescued and 'restored' on the orders of Francis Webb of the LNWR. It can now be found in the Science Museum. While it might be nice to think that it is the remains of *Catch Me Who Can*, there is no evidence to support the claim.[23]

Unlike his early locomotive, *Catch Me Who Can* did not have a geared drive nor a fly wheel and instead had direct drive to the rear wheels. *Catch Me Who Can* was displayed on a circular track in London, on a site close to the present University College London, in summer 1808.[24] It was announced in the London papers that the engine would 'be run against any mare, horse, or gelding that may be produced at the next October Meeting at Newmarket; the wagers are expected to be 10,000*l*; the engine is the favourite.'[25] The announcement of the wager continued during July. *The Times* advertised on July 19 that:

Racing Steam Engine – This surprising Engine will commence to exhibit her power

of speed to the public, THIS DAY, 11 o'clock ... Tickets of admission, 5s. each.

Sadly, however, things didn't go to plan as the *Morning Chronicle* noted the following day: the exhibition was to be postponed as the 'ground under the rail-way... being too soft and spongy, requires additional support'.

By the end of July, however, the London 'season' was over and as John Liffen has described, Trevithick postponed his exhibition runs until the fashionables of London had returned from Brighton and Bath and elsewhere.[26] The London and national press announced that the wager between engine and horse was to be re-run; the *Lancaster Gazette* described on October 1:

On the 23d ult. a great number of persons assembled on the ground near Russell-Square, London, to witness the action of a new machine for travelling without horses. It is impelled entirely by steam and is calculated to perform twenty miles an hour. The machine is principally made of iron, its body resembling a barrel; the fore part of which contains the water and in them rear is the furnace, which, while

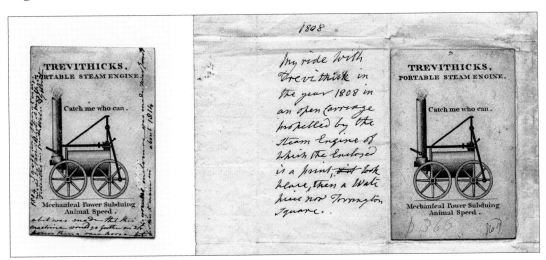

ABOVE: A ticket issued in 1808 for the public demonstration of *Catch Me Who Can*. It gives a reasonably accurate depiction of the locomotive, with a single cylinder immersed in the boiler with direct drive to the rear wheels. *(Science & Society Picture Library)*

TREVITHICK'S LONDON RAILWAY AND LOCOMOTIVE OF 1808. [W. J. Welch.]

ABOVE: A popular later Victorian depiction of *Catch Me Who Can* running on its demonstration track. This image formed the basis of a series of well-known fakes attributed to Thomas Rowlandson.

the machine is in motion, is fed by coals by one man, the only one employed to give it motion: a perpendicular pipe about ten feet long carries off the smoke. The machine runs round a groove, and seems self-directed, the wheels on one side being shorter than those on the other; it proceeds with great velocity, but the pace can be altered at pleasure.[27]

Thereafter, *Catch Me Who Can* disappears from the historical record. Despite a well-known depiction of the event reputedly by Thomas Rowlandson being frequently cited, that drawing is an early 20th century fake, but a drawing by John Claude Nattes has been identified as depicting the boiler and cylinder unit of *Catch Me Who Can* still on site near

Russell Square circa 1808.[28] A conjectural working replica was built at the workshops of the Severn Valley Railway in Bridgnorth in 2008.

WEST INDIA DOCKS AND PLYMOUTH BREAKWATER

These two locomotives were both of the do-anything 'steam Swiss army knife' type designed by Trevithick. That for the West India Docks (1804) was able to 'travel from ship to ship, to unload and to take up goods to the upper floors of the storehouses' and, in case of emergency, to act as a fire-pump 'to force water on the storehouses'. Whether the docks engine counts as a locomotive per se is not clear, but sadly for Trevithick

the London Docks authorities would not permit the engine to be set to work due to the fire risk.[29]

The Plymouth Breakwater engine (1812-1814) was designed to be able to both bore rock and draw waggons down to the quayside. Whilst it's clear that in March 1813 the 'engine for Plymouth will be put to break ground' as soon as Trevithick could find the time, an engine of some form was put to work as the cost of granite for the breakwater project fell from 2s 9d per ton to 1s just as Trevithick promised his engine would. As with the West India Docks locomotive, whether the Breakwater engine – whilst it was clearly self-moving – was rail-borne is unknown, as is their final appearance.[30]

ABOVE: A working replica of *Catch Me Who Can* was built in 2008 by the Trevithick 200 organisation. It is based at Bridgnorth on the Severn Valley Railway and occasionally steamed.

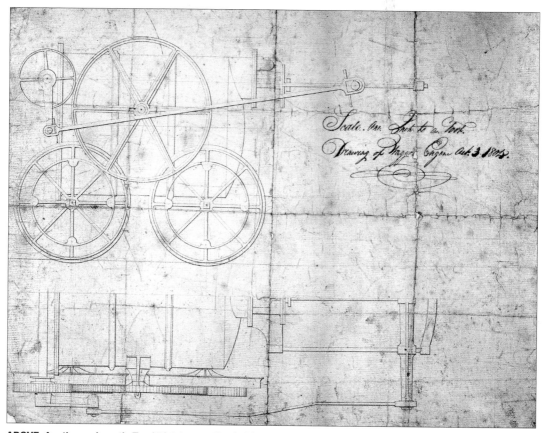

ABOVE: Another enigmatic Trevithick locomotive is his 'Waggon Engine' dated October 3,1804. Like the Gateshead locomotive, the cylinder is at the opposite end to the firebox. Also note the lack of a flywheel. *(Science & Society Picture Library)*

POSSIBLE TREVITHICK DESIGNS

There are several remaining possible Trevithick-inspired locomotives left to consider: the first is Chapman's Newcastle Locomotive of 1812 which may have in fact been a steam-powered element of the Chapman brothers' patent rope-making machinery. It used 'slightly indented wheels' like those specified in Hedley's 1813 patent as Chapman 'had no idea that weight and friction would give the wheels sufficient hold.' The second is *Black Billy* a single-cylinder locomotive with flywheel built for the Wylam Waggonway (Chapter 4). Christopher Blackett, the owner, had in 1809 attempted to persuade Trevithick to build him

a locomotive but Trevithick had declined. Certainly a locomotive was built and Nicholas Wood described it in 1825 as an experimental machine with an irregular motion which had 'a tendency to shake the machine to pieces', but it did work and 'for some time ... the whole of the coals was taken down the Rail-road by the use of this kind of engine'.

The single cylinder, flywheel and geared drive are clearly derived from Trevithick practice although it probably had a straight-rather than return-flue boiler. Another possible Trevithick-derived locomotive was built at Whitehaven around 1812 by Taylor Swainson (Chapter 3). Finally, an engine built for the Fatfield Colliery may simply have been a high-pressure stationary engine.[31]

Despite the failure of many of Trevithick's ideas – due to them literally being at the 'cutting edge' of the technology then available – and ending his days in poverty and obscurity, he pioneered the use of high pressure steam, showing that a compact high pressure steam engine could be adapted to both road and rail uses.

In his patent with Andrew Vivian in 1802 he established the use of two cylinders driving cranks at right angles; that such a vehicle could be propelled by adhesion alone; and in his Penydarren locomotive the blast pipe so crucial to the performance of the locomotive. Although his locomotives are regarded today as somewhat ephemeral, and not necessarily a commercial success, he laid the foundations for what was to come.

Chapter 2
Blenkinsop and Murray 1811-1815

The Middleton Railway in Leeds has many claims to national and international significance: It was the first railway to be built under the powers of an Act of Parliament (1758); the first standard gauge railway to be preserved and operated by volunteers (1959). It is the oldest continuously-at-work railway in the world... and it was here that engineers successfully solved the problem of making a locomotive light enough so that it would not break the track but also capable of moving a useful load.

In 1812 John Blenkinsop and Matthew Murray introduced the first successful, commercial steam locomotive using a unique rack and pinion drive.

JOHN BLENKINSOP

The Middleton Railway had been opened in 1758 to carry coals from pits owned by the Brandling family at Middleton Park (a few

ABOVE: Drawn and published by George Walker in 1814 *The Collier* depicts the Middleton colliery and its railway, with a Blenkinsop and Murray locomotive rumbling past with a heavy train.

miles south of Leeds) down to staithes on the River Aire.

Though the wooden rails laid in 1758 had been replaced in the 1790s with iron rails supported on stone blocks, making the railway more efficient to work, the rising cost of horses and their fodder soon caused problems.

In 1808 the Middleton viewer ('manager' in modern parlance) died, and the owner Charles John Brandling (1769-1826) chose as his replacement a young man already working at his Tyneside pits: John Blenkinsop (1783-1831). Blenkinsop's main task was to modernise the whole system of working at Middleton and thus reduce operating costs.

He began work there in October 1814 on a salary of £400. Born in Felling on Tyneside, he had been trained at Brandling's Felling pit.

When Blenkinsop arrived at Middleton the line was worked by horses on two level sections which were linked by a 1 in 18 incline known as Todd's Run that was powered by a horse gin. Blenkinsop re-routed the waggonway to avoid some of the steepest gradients and iron rails were obtained from the Low Moor company of Bradford.

The next step was to improve the means of motive power, and it is possible Blenkinsop had witnessed the Trevithick locomotive constructed at John Whinfield's foundry at Gateshead (Chapter 1) in 1805, which sparked the germ of the idea of using steam locomotion at Middleton.

The problem faced by Blenkinsop was making a locomotive light enough so that it did not break the brittle cast iron rails then in use. But, in order to make a locomotive sufficiently light so as not to destroy the track it ran on, there would be the second problem of adhesion. Thus, 'aided by the advice and suggestions … of Mr John Straker' Blenkinsop devised a rack-and-pinion

ABOVE: Matthew Murray, the Leeds-based engineer who was the main rival to Boulton and Watt of Birmingham. Together with John Blenkinsop he built the first commercially successful steam locomotive.

system of railways, whereby a lightweight locomotive would wind itself along the track using a cogged wheel engaging in a rack rail. This idea was patented on April 10, 1811. Registered as Patent No. 3431, Blenkinsop's specification only covers the rack rail and wheel, but not the design of the steam engine, merely adding that steam was to be preferred 'to any other first mover'.[32]

MATTHEW MURRAY

In order to build his 'patent steam carriages' Blenkinsop turned to the Leeds firm of Fenton, Murray & Wood of the 'Round Foundry' who had established themselves as makers of mill machinery and steam engines of sufficient quality as to rival those of Boulton and Watt, and Murray had worked closely with Marc Brunel in supplying steam engines and machinery for the Admiralty.

Matthew Murray (1765-1826) was born in Newcastle upon Tyne, and had been apprenticed as a whitesmith but soon became a journeyman mechanic at a Darlington flax mill. He moved to Leeds in 1789 to work for John Marshall. In Leeds, Murray designed and patented machinery for working in linen mills. Together with David Wood he established Fenton, Murray & Wood in 1791. An intense rivalry built up between the 'Round Foundry' and Boulton and Watt, with James Watt jr buying up land around the 'Round Foundry' to prevent any further expansion, and even attempting to bribe some of the Leeds foundrymen for technical information.[33]

The final design of the 'steam carriage' was clearly the work of Murray and it would influence the design of the next generation of pioneering locomotives. Murray had in 1802 designed and patented a lightweight portable steam engine. This was a four horsepower single-cylinder machine; sadly the patent was found to infringe on that of Boulton and Watt and was revoked in 1803, but at least one engine was made. A second portable engine appeared in 1805. Fenton, Murray and Wood built a Trevithick-type high pressure engine for the paddle steamer *l'Actif* in 1811, the same year that they built their first locomotive.[34] It was a single-cylinder condensing engine, probably based on the small, portable engine design of 1805:

When we saw Mr. Blinkinsop's [sic] first trial he employed a small condensing engine, but finding the water to grow so hot that he gained but little by the condensation, he applied a high-pressure engine with a wrought-iron boiler, and two cylinders in it acting upon separate cranks, so as to produce a constant action to advance the carriage without the necessity of using a fly-wheel.[35]

THE FIRST COMMERCIAL LOCOMOTIVE

Murray's design of locomotive was ground-breaking. Whereas Trevithick's early schemes had used a single cylinder and fly-wheel (*Catch Me Who Can* notwithstanding), by using two cylinders working out of phase Murray has dispensed with the cumbersome flywheel which meant the locomotive could run far more steadily and also re-start from a stationary position. This idea had apparently been arrived at separately by both Murray and Trevithick in 1802.[36]

By using two cylinders, Murray also doubled the power output. He placed the cylinders along the centre line of the boiler, and immersed within it to keep them warm to prevent the steam condensing in the cylinders. Here, Murray was borrowing from Trevithick and Vivian's patent of 1801, and would establish the basic form of locomotive as developed by George Stephenson and others.[37] It is not clear whether the cylinders on the first locomotive were double-acting or not as the crank is shown as being set at 180° in the earliest technical description of these engines; a letter from Blenkinsop (dated March 1814) and published in *The Monthly Magazine* of June 1814, however, records that the cranks were set at 90° implying a change to double-acting cylinders.[38] The cylinders had an 8in bore and 24in stroke, later copied by George Stephenson in his earliest locomotives. The long stroke (although short compared with Trevithick's practice) however, was wasteful of steam.[39]

Each piston rod was controlled by two guides and crossheads, and two connecting rods transferred the power via cranks to a drive shaft which carried a spur pinion mounted

ABOVE: This model of a Blenkinsop and Murray locomotive was probably made by or for John Blenkinsop in or around 1812. It is currently on display at Leeds City Museum.

centrally on each shaft, which engaged with a spur wheel (of twice the diameter) fixed to a central shaft on which the side-mounted rack wheel was fitted.[40]

The problem with using a rack wheel on one side was uneven torque, and indeed Murray expressed during 1813 that he would have preferred to have used a central rack wheel but had been forced to use a side-mounted rack so as to leave the space between the rails clear for shunting horses. The side rack

'did very well as a cheap method for trying the scheme, but certainly is not calculated for practice'. The side-mounted rack wheel 'cause[d] the wheels of the engine to wear away very fast, and proportionately the rails, and this I am afraid we will discover to a greater extent than imagined'.[41]

Even though Murray had invented and patented the D-shaped slide valve in 1802, steam was distributed using four-way plug cocks exactly as Trevithick had done.

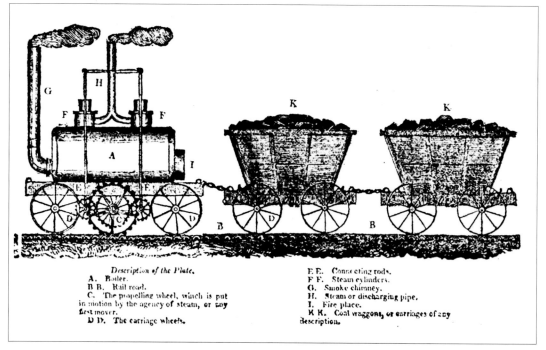

Description of the Plate.
A. Boiler.
B B. Rail road.
C. The propelling wheel, which is put in motion by the agency of steam, or any first mover.
D D. The carriage wheels.
E E. Connecting rods.
F F. Steam cylinders.
G. Smoke chimney.
H. Steam or discharging pipe.
I. Fire place.
K K. Coal waggons, or carriages of any description.

ABOVE: A detailed, early depiction of one of the Middleton locomotives, from the *Monthly Magazine* for June 1814.

The cocks were oscillated through 90° via rocking-levers mounted on either end of the boiler, driven via tappets mounted on the driven axle which knocked against an iron frame as the axle revolved providing the reciprocating motion. This valve gear was uni-directional, so hand levers were provided so that the engineman could reverse the engine manually.[42]

The boiler was cast iron (emulating Trevithick), was oval in cross-section, cast in two halves and bolted together. A single wrought iron flue passed through the boiler. The chimney was cast iron. There were two spring-loaded safety valves set to 55psi, and the tension of the coil spring could be adjusted with a nut, which would have fatal repercussions for George Hutchinson when *Salamanca* blew up in 1818 after he had apparently tampered with the safety valves. In spring 1813 Murray was musing with the idea of using a wrought iron boiler in

order to reduce the weight of the engine and increase the capacity of the boiler to 'enable the engine to go a greater distance with one charging of water'.[43]

The Middleton locomotives were intended to work intermittently over short distances being restricted to working the two 'levels', and as Blenkinsop wrote to John Watson of Newcastle only a few weeks after they began working in summer 1812, the engines were at first stopped at the end of each run and 'recharged', the boiler pressure being released each time:

The water used per hour is 9 solid feet or 55 gals – but in consequence of letting off the steam to charge and filling with cold water each journey will require more fuel and water than if boiling water was put into the boiler by means of a force pump or elevated cistern. I intend to feed with hot water tomorrow but it will be a week or ten days before I can raise a cistern so as to fill the boiler without discharging the steam.[44]

Two years later, Blenkinsop noted that the engines were using 50 gallons of water per hour and 8cwt of coal 'will supply the machine twelve hours', and that 'The Engine will go 5 miles without filling the boiler'. By 1825 there was a pump to refill the boiler 'midway of the rail road.'[45] In other words, the boiler capacity was based upon the time the water would last, rather than on the supply of steam required. Thus, they were 'single fill' boilers, and this arrangement was later adopted by Blenkinsop and Murray for their later locomotives for the Kenton & Coxlodge Railway and the Orrell Colliery, and also by William Chapman. This is surprising, given that Trevithick's high pressure stationary and locomotive engines had been fitted with feed-pumps.[46] The American Zachariah Allen who visited in 1825 noted 'The boiler is replenished with water from a pump placed midway of the rail road, where the engineer, at every trip, stops a few moments'.[47] These locomotives never had any tenders, which again reinforces that they were 'single fill' in terms of operation, being worked in short 'bursts' of operation.

Exhaust steam initially vented directly into the atmosphere but this was found to scare the horses, so instead a wooden silencer with a pipe at the top to allow the steam escape was fitted. This pipe was offset 'so as the steam not blow into it from the cylinders but against the roof of the box'. There was also a drain pipe 'to carry off the condensed water' to prevent water building up in the box and 'choking' the cocks.[48]

The boilers and cylinders were clad with wood. There was a problem, however, with condensed exhaust steam – due to the long stroke cylinders, there would be a lot of condensate in the exhaust – damaging the iron work and one suggestion was the use of

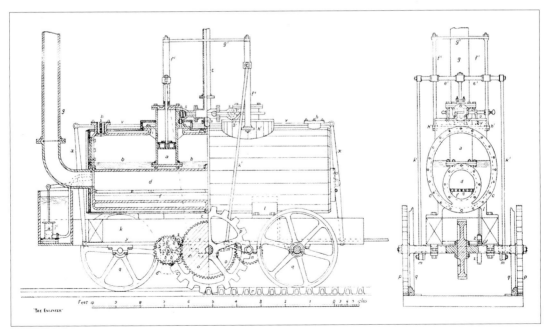

ABOVE: A French technical drawing of one of the Middleton locomotives, published in 1815. The Middleton colliery and its railway gained international interest after the introduction of steam locomotion.

a canvas awning to 'keep the iron dry from the Steam'. By 1817 black lead was being purchased to keep the engines rust-free.[49]

VIVAT LEODIS

The first practical, commercial use of steam locomotion was in June 1812. The *Leeds Mercury* on Saturday, June 7, 1812 records:

On Wednesday last a highly interesting experiment was made with a machine constructed by Messrs. Fenton, Murray, and Wood, ...under the Direction of Mr John Blenkinsop, the Patentee, for the purpose of substituting the agency of steam for the use of horses in the conveyance of coals on the Iron-railway from the mines of J. C. Brandling ... to Leeds. This machine is ... of four horses' power, which, with the assistance of cranks turning a cog-wheel, and iron cogs placed at one side of the rail-way, is capable of moving ... at the speed of ten miles an hour. At four o'clock in the afternoon, the machine ran from the Coal-staith to the top of Hunslet-Moor, where six, and afterwards eight wagons of coal, each weighing 3 tons, were hooked to the back part. With this immense weight, to which, as it approached the town, was super-added about 50 of the spectators mounted upon the wagons, it set off on its return to the Coal-staith, and performed the journey, a distance of about a mile and a half ... in 23 minutes. The experiment ... was witnessed by thousands of spectators, was crowned by with complete success.

With the price of horses and their fodder at an all time high, the *Mercury* continued:

The use of 50 horses will be dispensed with, and the corn necessary for the consumption of, at least, 200 men, saved, we cannot but forebear to hail the invention as of vast public utility. The eight waggons of coals brought to Leeds at the launching of the machine, was

now subjoin a Drawing of the Machine and toothed Rail-way, accompanied by an abstract of the Specification of the Patent granted on the 10th of April, 1811, to the Inventor, Mr. JOHN BLENKINSOP, of Middleton, near this place.

DESCRIPTION OF PLATE.

A. Boiler.
B. B. B. Mr. Blenkinsop's Patent Road Rack and Wheel.
C. C. Crank Rods.
D. D. Steam Cylinder.
E. Discharging Pipe.
F. Smoke Chimney.
G. Fire Door.
Scale, 1-eighth of an Inch.

SPECIFICATION.—*First*, There is placed upon the road over which the conveyance is to be made, a toothed Rack or longitudinal piece of cast-iron, having the teeth or protuberances standing either upwards, or downwards, or sideways, in any re-

ABOVE: Perhaps the earliest newspaper depiction of a steam locomotive: Blenkinsop's 'patent steam carriage' from the *Leeds Mercury* July 18, 1812.

by order or Mr. Blenkinsop, presented to the General Infirmary.

During 1814 Blenkinsop claimed that one of his patent engines was capable of doing the work of 16 horses in a 12 hour period, which represented a saving of £1200 between locomotives and horses. In a detailed and lengthy letter to John Watson at Willington, he adumbrated that the cost of working the Kenton and Coxlodge Railway on Tyneside using 81 horses cost £9453 per year, while the cost of replacing them with five locomotives was £1458 4s, representing a cost saving of a whopping £7995. Of course this had to be off-set with the cost of relaying one side of the railway with the cast-iron rack rails.[50]

The *Mercury* of July 18, 1812 carried a wood-cut of the engine – perhaps the first newspaper depiction of a steam locomotive. A few weeks later the same paper described that:

Mr Blenkinsop's Machine is now in full activity. On Thursday it made seven journies each way from Hunslet-Moor to the Coal Staithe and back again, and in those journies brought down 102 waggons of coals, each weighing about three tons. The journey both ways is a distance of about two miles and a half, and one of these journies was performed in fifty minutes, taking up twenty and bringing down twenty full waggons.

Blenkinsop wrote in August 1812 that 'my Patent Steam Carriage is daily at work and is capable of moving 20 coal waggons each weighing 3½ tons at the rate of 3½ miles an hour'. The total load was 74 tons including the locomotive, suggesting it only weighed around four tons. He also confirmed the press reportage that 'One Journey with 20 waggons (1½ miles each) was performed in 50 minutes'.[51] When James Walker and John Rastrick visited Middleton in 1829 on behalf of the Liverpool and Manchester Railway they observed one of the engines hauling a load of 110 tons at a speed of 2 – 3½ mph on the level.

The first of the Middleton locomotives was named *Salamanca* after the recent Allied victory in the Peninsular War. The pair of them were paid for in December, costing £350 each plus a royalty payment of £30 to William West, owner of the Trevithick patent for high pressure steam. The first driver was probably John Hewitt who was paid 2s 6d per day and later William Lister who was paid 5s per day. Another early driver was George Butler who lost his hand in an accident: reports described how 'while supplying the fire with coal' he fell from his 'platform' and had his 'hand entangled in the machinery, his

right hand was severed from his body before he could be extracted'.

MECHANISED TRANSPORT

The first pair of locomotives were worked on the level between Todd's Run Incline on Hunslet Moor and the staithes on the River Aire. In one of his letters, Blenkinsop implies his locomotives may have been intended to have worked up the incline, and indeed stated in 1818 that one of his machines could haul a load of '15 tons up a hill rising two inches in a yard'.

An additional locomotive was purchased in late 1813 and the fourth engine was delivered in March 1815. The names of the locomotives are unclear: certainly the only names mentioned contemporaneously were *Salamanca* and *Lord Wellington*. E K Scott in his unreliable 1920s biography of Matthew Murray also names *Prince Regent* and *Marquis Wellesley,* but provides no source.

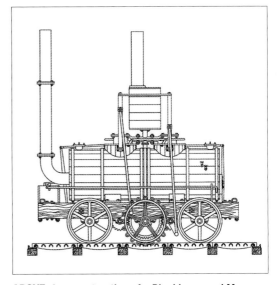

ABOVE: A reconstruction of a Blenkinsop and Murray locomotive by Stuart Saint. Note the large 'silencer' box above the exhaust pipe to lessen the noise and prevent horses being scared as well as the feed water tank mounted at the front of the locomotive. *(Stuart Saint)*

Thus, from November 1815 two engines worked on each level. What was probably the world's first engine shed was built in 1815 at a cost of £25.[52]

Introduction of steam locomotives on the Middleton required all the infrastructure to be upgraded: new cast iron rails were laid, costing £1000. Coupling chains proved too weak and had to be strengthened. So too the wooden-bodied waggons, which were quickly replaced by ones with iron-frames. Later waggons had trap-door bottoms to allow them to rapidly unload their cargo of coal at the Leeds coal staithes. By 1825 the whole process of getting coal out of the mine and transporting it to the staithes was entirely mechanised, 'not once subjected to the expense of … manual labour'.

Not everyone welcomed the introduction of steam locomotion, however. Unemployment in Leeds was high thanks to increasing mechanisation of the textile trade, and as we have seen, mechanisation of the Middleton's transport needs resulted in the laying off of men and horses. Thus it's not surprising that in December 1812 Luddites carried out an act of sabotage on the railway. John Blenkinsop offered a reward of 50 guineas to apprehend the culprits.[53]

SUCCESS IN THE NORTH

Success of the Blenkinsop/Murray locomotives was widely reported in the domestic press, and in 1818 Blenkinsop wrote that his engines were 'daily' at work at the Wellington (sic, Willington) colliery of John Watson; at the Kenton and Coxlodge collieries (both on Tyneside) and at the Orrell Colliery, near Wigan.

John Watson, who was the viewer at the Kenton and Coxlodge (K&C) Colliery and Willington Colliery, was an early advocate of them. The K&C was re-laid with new heavier

rails and with Blenkinsop's patent rack rails to allow the use of locomotives during early 1813; the first engine for the K&C had originally been intended for the Middleton.

Murray did not really approve of this loan, as the engine's boiler was 'calculated only for Mr Blenkinsop's short distance' and being of the 'single fill' type, would need to be frequently refilled with hot water on the longer K&C system.[54] Furthermore, because the Middleton used a gauge of 4ft 1in and the K&C 4ft 7½in the engine would require redesign to suit the wider gauge.

The *Morning Chronicle* reported that the first locomotive began work on September 2, 1813 and was capable of moving a load of 70 tons on the level at 3½mph. Watson had been so impressed by the first engine that in October he placed an order for two locomotives from Fenton, Murray & Wood, whilst the locomotive diverted from the Middleton to the K&C was only finally paid for in June 1814 (£354 2s 4d).[55] When it was rumoured the K&C might adopt adhesion worked locomotives on the 'Killingworth plan', Blenkinsop chided his sceptics: 'Do you think the Killingworth engine will travel up hill or on a level during wet or frost?'. His engines could work through the worst of weathers, 'and was not impeded during the great falls of snow'. Sadly in May 1815 there was a lengthy legal dispute with a neighbouring colliery and the locomotives were laid off. Brandling purchased Coxlodge Colliery in 1817, but locomotive haulage was not revived.[56] It is interesting to note that one of George Stephenson's brothers, Robert (1788-1837) was employed as an 'engineman' on the Kenton and Coxlodge.[57]

Three locomotives were built under licence by the Haigh Foundry on behalf of Robert Daglish of the Orrell Colliery near Wigan. Indeed, John Clarke, a wealthy

ABOVE: A fanciful German depiction, probably inspired by Thomas Gray's *Observations on a General Iron Rail-Way* (1820) of a Blenkinsop and Murray locomotive pulling a passenger carriage. Two Middleton-type locomotives were built in Germany. *(Beamish Museum)*

Liverpool banker and colliery proprietor, had approached Blenkinsop offering a one-off payment of £500 for the use of his patent locomotives and rail throughout Lancashire. This met with a flat-out refusal from Blenkinsop, but he did agree to travel to Wigan or Liverpool to meet Clark and discuss the matter further, eventually writing a detailed cost benefit statement.

One of the Orrell Colliery locomotives was supposedly built as an adhesion machine, foregoing the expense of the patent rack system. As early as November 1776 a horse-worked waggonway had been in use at Orrell Colliery, laid with wooden rails to a gauge of four feet. It was relaid with iron rails in 1812. Known locally as the 'Yorkshire Horse', the Orrell locomotives were larger than the Middleton versions and had wrought iron rather than cast iron boilers. The Orrell locomotives, like those in Leeds, had a long

service life, upwards of 30 years where they were capable of shifting loads of up to 90 tons at 3mph, with one locomotive doing the work of 14 horses saving £500 per annum. The last one was broken up as recently as the 1920s, having been used to power a hay cutter at the colliery stables.[58] A Blenkinsop locomotive was also built for the Nantyglo colliery in south Wales in 1813 and was at work until 1830.[59]

INTERNATIONAL RECOGNITION

Success of the mechanisation of the Middleton's transportation needs soon aroused international interest; as we have seen French observers visited circa1815. Two Prussian engineers visited Britain circa 1814, and saw Blenkinsop-type locomotives at work in Leeds and Newcastle. Dr S H Spiker, the King of Prussia's librarian,

ABOVE: Original Blenkinsop patent rack rail preserved at the Middleton Railway, Leeds. *(Anthony Dawson/Middleton Railway Trust)*

ABOVE: A replica rack wheel was cast in 2012 to mark the bicentenary of steam locomotion both on the Middleton Railway and nationally. *(Anthony Dawson/Middleton Railway Trust)*

visited and reported in 1815, while the future Tsar Nicholas I of Russia visited in 1816 – Murray sending him a working model of one of the locomotives. Two Americans, William Strickland and Zachariah Allen, visited in 1825 and two more Prussian engineers Ernst Von Dechen and Karl Von Oeynhausen in 1826-27. Blenksinop-type locomotives were the first to operate in mainland Europe. Two were built in Prussia 1816-1819. The Prussian state had sponsored the 'secret' visit of Johann Friedrich Krigar, Director of the Royal Iron Foundry in Berlin to the Middleton Railway in 1814. Two years later he was commissioned to build a Blenkinsop-type locomotive which was used to to transport coal to the ironworks at Königshütte in Silesia. A second, larger, locomotive was built in 1819 for coal mines in Saarland. It was used sporadically until 1821 when it was laid up and exhibited outside the colliery offices. It was broken up for scrap in 1836. Another Blenkinsop locomotive was built for Joseph Frederic Braconier, proprietor of a colliery at Horloz near Liege in modern-day Belgium, around 1817.[60]

Blenkinsop and Murray's locomotives, although dismissed by the likes of Samuel Smiles, were the world's first commercially successful steam locomotives and their design would go on to influence the work of George Stephenson and others who would come later.

Blenkinsop and Murray revolutionised the working of the Middleton Colliery, the mechanisation of the local coal industry going hand in hand with the mechanisation of other industries at the time, particularly textiles. While Trevithick had laid the foundations for the locomotive, it was Blenkinsop and Murray who were the first to develop its commercial potential and create the first truly successful steam locomotive.

Chapter 3
Mechanical horses and steam elephants 1812-1822

BRUNTON'S MECHANICAL HORSE

Although Blenkinsop and Murray had seemingly solved the twin problems of building a locomotive light enough so that it did not break the track and was also able to haul a useful load, this did not stop other engineers coming up with their own solutions, including the use of mechanical legs or the locomotive hauling itself along a chain.

William Brunton (1777-1851) was a Scottish engineer who had been trained by his father (a watch and clock maker) and grandfather (a coal viewer). In 1790 he started work as a millwright at a cotton mill in New Lanark but in 1796 moved to Birmingham to work for Boulton and Watt.

He moved, in 1808, to the Butterley Ironworks at Crich in Derbyshire in 1808 as 'senior engineer' and worked there until 1815. Working for the Butterley Ironworks he 'established the manufacture of engines… he made some of the first engines used [in steam boats] on the Humber and Trent, and was amongst the first on the Mersey'.[61] While at Butterley he would have no doubt supervised the construction of William Chapman's first locomotive in 1813 (below).

He was an experienced engineer and his most remarkable contribution to the history of the locomotive was his 'mechanical horse', which was patented in July 1813. Brunton's 'mechanical horse' was not necessarily designed as a railway locomotive. It was intended to replace the horse in a variety of situations including towing canal boats or even on roads.[62] If having a steam engine propel itself using legs is considered eccentric, David Gordon in 1824 and the Quaker engineer Goldsworthy Gurney in 1825 both proposed steam road coaches which used legs.[63] Thomas Meade of Sculcoates, Hull, also patented a steam engine which was propelled by legs in 1813.[64]

The 'mechanical horse' was built by Brunton as a private venture and first tried on the tramway at Crich at the end of November 1813. The wrought-iron boiler was only 5ft 6ins long and 3ft diameter, and according to Brunton was 'capable of sustaining an internal pressure of four or five hundred pounds on the square inch.' There was a single cylinder (6 x 24 inches) and the whole machine, including water, weighed 45cwt. It had a speed of 2½ mph and was probably about 6hp. It cost £240.

Flushed with success, he built a second two cylinder version for Nesham & Co of the Newbottle Colliery near Newcastle, costing £540. It was built at Butterley and sent north

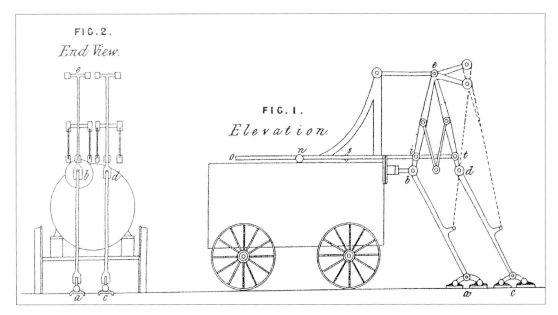

ABOVE: Extracts from Brunton's 1813 patent application for his mechanical traveller. In the form depicted the design could not possibly work due the lack of a fulcrum to support the 'legs'.

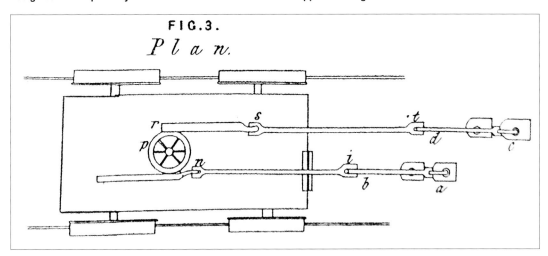

via canal and river to Gainsborough and then onwards by coastal lighter, arriving by October 19, 1814.[65] According to Brunton 'Its legs moved alternately, and the length of the step being 6 feet, each propulsion moved the machine forward 12 feet' and it was capable of moving a load up a gradient of 1 in 36.[66] The 'mechanical traveller' must have worked well enough for other colliery viewers to have recommended its adoption,

and for Edward Pease to be surprised that George Stephenson's first locomotive didn't go by legs![67]

The Globe of London reported: 'The proprietors had provided a locomotive steam engine for the purpose of drawing 10 or 12 coal waggons to the staithe at one time'. A 'great many' persons had gathered on Monday July 23, 1815 to witness the scene:

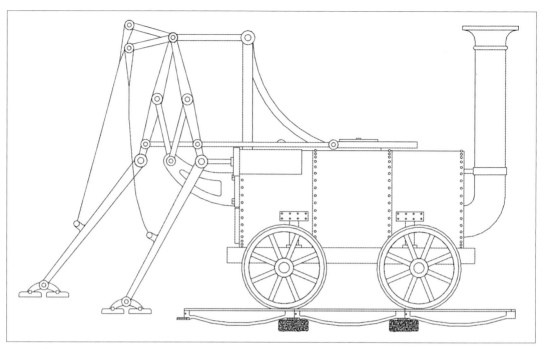

ABOVE: A reconstruction of Brunton's later two-cylinder locomotive for the Newbottle Colliery, including the vital pivot-point so that the legs work. *(Stuart Saint)*

Unfortunately, just as it was going off, the boiler of the machine burst. The engineman was dashed to pieces, and his mangled remains blown one hundred and fourteen yards; the top the boiler (nine feet square, weight nineteen hundred weight) was blown one hundred yards; and the two cylinders ninety yards. A little boy was also thrown a great distance. By this accident fifty-seven persons were killed and wounded, of whom eleven were dead on Sunday night, and several remain dangerous ill.[68]

The accident was blamed on the engineman screwing down the safety valve:

As there were several viewers and owners there, he would make her go in grand style, and he got upon the boiler to loose the screw of the safety valve, but being overheated, it unfortunately exploded.[69]

The explosion of the 'mechanical horse' was reported country-wide and even resurfaced two years later concerning the dangers of high pressure steam.[70] Sadly, this was the second accident at Newbottle in as many months: on the afternoon of June 2, 1815 an underground explosion of 'mine damp' resulted in the death of 24 men and 28 boys, it taking two days to recover the bodies.[71]

Following the Newbottle explosion, Brunton left the Butterley Ironworks (it isn't clear if the two are related) and became managing partner at the Eagle Foundry in Birmingham. Despite the eccentricity of his 'mechanical traveller' and its untimely demise, Brunton continued as a well-respected engineer and was involved with the promotion of several railway projects, including the London & Birmingham and Great Western.[72]

CHAPMAN AND BUDDLE

Another attempt at solving the weight and adhesion problem was made by John Buddle and his business partner William Chapman.

Buddle (1773-1843) of Newcastle was perhaps the foremost colliery viewer of his age. He was involved with the development of early railways both in Britain and overseas. He was a Unitarian and associated with the Rev William Turner of Newcastle.

William Chapman (1749-1832) was a Quaker but was expelled from his meeting for reneging on a marriage agreement, which put him in bad standing with other Quakers such as the Peases. He was a canal engineer 'of considerable reputation' specialising in harbour and drainage schemes as well as skew bridges, such as at Kildare in Ireland. Together with his brother Edward (1762-1847) he had taken out about a dozen patents between 1798 and 1812, including one for a rope making machine. The Chapman brothers patented their locomotive in 1812 – the cost of the patent being paid for by Buddle – and a pamphlet was published in Newcastle the same year. Indeed, when the engine was tried at Heaton Colliery where Buddle was a partner and the viewer, it was Buddle who paid for the fitting up of the engine, the chains for the track and 'railway kettle' for filling its boiler with hot water. Buddle also supervised the trial and modifications to the engine.[73]

The Chapman brothers' patent of December 1812 included the provision of bogies in order to spread the weight of a locomotive over a wider wheelbase so as not to damage the brittle cast iron rails or plates then in use.

The Chapmans' locomotive was a curious machine which hauled itself along a chain supported in forks down the centre of the track. The engine consisted of a return-flue boiler with two cylinders immersed on its centre line, the piston rod guided by slide bars and a cross-head after the manner of Blenkinsop and Murray (Chapter 2).

ABOVE: John Buddle, the leading coal viewer of the North East; he also had interests elsewhere including Whitehaven in Cumbria.

ABOVE: The Quaker civil engineer William Chapman, who with his brother took out a dozen patents in as many years and who worked closely with Buddle in developing a practical locomotive.

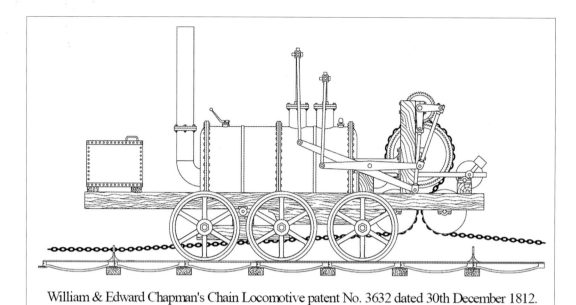

William & Edward Chapman's Chain Locomotive patent No. 3632 dated 30th December 1812.
Built by the Butterley Company and used at Heaton Colliery in 1813.

ABOVE: A reconstruction of Chapman and Buddle's patent chain locomotive of December 1812. Built by the Butterley Iron Co for the Heaton Colliery, the locomotive hauled itself along a chain elevated down the centre of the track. *(Stuart Saint)*

The locomotive was built by the Butterley Ironworks, was completed by September 1813 and under trial on the Heaton waggon way in October. It was apparently demonstrated on the Lambton waggonway in early 1814. This first Heaton engine was taken off the waggonway following a colliery disaster and put to winding and pumping, never to return to the rails. An unimpressed John Blenkinsop referred to the chain-haulage locomotive as 'mechanical larceny'.[74]

In 1820 Buddle purchased the Lambton chain locomotive to use on a new line he was constructing at Heaton, and there it underwent further trials. Buddle had the locomotive rebuilt as an adhesion machine: the boiler was lengthened by three feet and fitted with a straight-flue, and it was converted from eight wheels to four and mounted on a single frame rather than bogies. The wheels were coupled by chain. This rebuilding was

probably carried out by Joseph Smith who was the enginewright at Heaton.[75]

A second locomotive, this time worked by adhesion, was designed by Chapman and Buddle and put to work in December 1814. The *Tyne Mercury* reported on January 3, 1815:

On Wednesday week, a locomotive engine built by Mr Phineas Crowther, was set to work on the waggon-way of John George Lambton esq. It drew after it eighteen loaded coal waggons (weight about 54 tons) up a gentle ascent rising five sixteenths of an inch to a yard, and went nearly at a rate of four miles an hour. The engine was mounted upon eight wheels, according to a patent granted to Messrs. Wm. and Edw. Chapman, by means of which the weight is so far reduced upon each wheel, as to avoid the expense of relaying the ways with stronger rails.[76]

Phineas Crowther (1763-1818) of the Ouseburn Foundry, Newcastle had been in partnership with John Whinfield (Chapter 1) until 1808, and had patented a stationary steam engine, in 1800, of which the Weatherill engine, preserved at the National Railway Museum, York, is an example of the type.

Although traditionally associated with John Buddle, it appears Chapman was keen to publicise his locomotive and generate orders on his own cognizance – including in South Wales, offering one of his patent engines to Ironmaster Benjamin Hall MP (1778-1817) in March 1815 for £400.[77]

WHITEHAVEN

Another eight-wheeler was built for the Croft Pit Waggonway at Whitehaven in 1816. It was ordered by John Peile, the Earl of Lonsdale's colliery agent, who was certainly interested in locomotives.

In March 1815 he had written to John Buddle inquiring about his experiments 'in perfecting your Union Moving Steam Wagon' and in November 1815 wrote again asking 'what progress have you made with your Travelling Engine? We are still interested'. Finally an order was placed with Phineas Crowther via Buddle on November 20, 1816. The boiler, chimney, wheels and feed-water cistern were to be made in Whitehaven and the remainder from Chapman's patterns.

Two contemporary drawings of this locomotive exist, and Jim Rees has presented

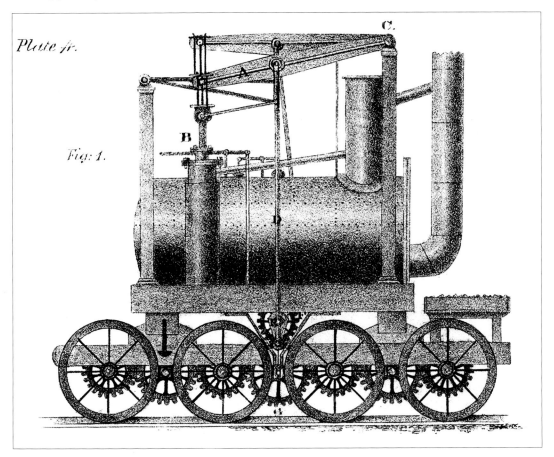

ABOVE: Chapman's 1812 patent also included the bogie ('truck' in American parlance). His and Buddle's locomotive for Lambton Colliery was adhesion-worked and carried on two four-wheel bogies. *(Beamish Museum)*

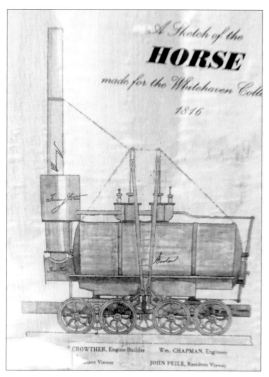

ABOVE: A reconstruction of the eight-wheeler (mounted on two four-wheel bogies) Chapman and Buddle locomotive erected by Taylor Swainson for work at Whitehaven, Cumbria in 1816. It was out of use by 1819.

a reconstruction of it. It had a straight flue boiler and two cylinders (circa 9 x 24 inches) immersed on the centre line of the boiler working down to cranks set 90° apart. There was a feed water heater around the base of the chimney.[78]

The engine was erected at Whitehaven by the colliery enginewright Taylor Swainson (who was traditionally credited with having 'invented' it). It should also be noted that Swainson was a friend of Buddle, and that Buddle often visited Whitehaven in his capacity as consulting viewer. The locomotive was tried on the Croft waggonway in 1817, but even though it was mounted on eight wheels it was found to damage the track so badly that it was laid up and converted into a stationary pumping and winding engine.[79]

In 1819 Buddle gave up many of his colliery interests to become viewer to Lord Londonderry who had collieries at Rainton and Penshaw in County Durham. A 'travelling engine for leading coals' was built by Joseph Smith (who had moved from Heaton) for Rainton Colliery in 1822 and was apparently at work for a few years but broke rails and suffered wheel slip. A final engine was perhaps also the first crane locomotive, built in the same year for work on Lord Londonderry's new country house at Wynard. It may also be the same engine used on construction work at Seaham Harbour, where William Chapman was engineer and Buddle the manager, in 1828.[80]

THE *STEAM ELEPHANT*

A six-wheel Chapman & Buddle engine was built 1814-1815 for Wallsend Colliery, the premiere mine in the northeast coal field, and another at which Buddle was the viewer.

The colliery was in the process of being revitalised and modernised by William Chapman but the money ran out and was instead purchased by William Russell who became the 'richest mere commoner' in England. The locomotive was supplied as a kit of parts by Hawks of Gateshead and was put to work early in 1816, but was transferred to another of Buddle's collieries at Washington, where it was again laid aside when Matthias Dunn saw it in May 1816. It is likely it damaged the rails even though (William) Losh cast iron rails had been purchased in 1821, but had not necessarily been laid. This was *Steam Elephant*, probably the first 0-6-0 locomotive, which became the workhorse of Britain's railways.[81]

The existence of *Steam Elephant* was only known through the payments to Hawks, until Jim Rees the keeper of industry at Beamish Museum was able to tie existing depictions of a geared six-wheel locomotive with that at Wallsend and in the process discovered a highly detailed oil painting of the locomotive in use.[82]

A full size working replica was built at Beamish Museum. The locomotive had many similarities with the Whitehaven example and the Blenkinsop and Murray influence is strong and self-evident. It has two cylinders immersed in the boiler, the piston rod being guided by slide bars and a cross-head. The cylinders were 8 or 9 x 24 inches, as used by Blenkinsop and Murray, so too the 2:1 gear reduction. Steam was distributed via slide valves worked by eccentrics, although apparently early locomotives had used four-way cocks and 'tumbler' valve gear as Blenkinsop and Murray had done. The

eccentrics were mounted on the two powered lay-shafts, and worked the valves, as at Middleton, with rocking beams fore and after to work horizontal shafts along the top of the boiler.

There was a feed-water heater around the chimney as well as a water pump, but there are no contemporary depictions of the locomotive ever having a tender. Its limited heating surface and small boiler suggest that *Steam Elephant*, like Blenkinsop and Murray's locomotives, were not designed for continuous operation although the water pump would argue that *Steam Elephant* was not of 'single fill' operation.[83]

As Jim Rees concluded, the stories of the *Steam Elephant*, and indeed Chapman and Buddle, have been traditionally often

ABOVE: A full-size working replica of Chapman and Buddle's *Steam Elephant* was built by Beamish Museum in 2001 in a project led by Jim Rees. The replica is largely based on a detailed oil painting of the locomotive circa 1816. It is similar to Blenkinsop and Murray's locomotives, albeit relying on adhesion.

ABOVE: The fireman checks his fire; crew provision in the early days was rudimentary at best.

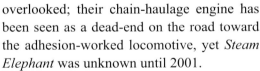

ABOVE: *Steam Elephant's* water tank being filled. Located around the chimney, the hot exhaust gasses heat the water in the tank acting as a pre-heater.

ABOVE: *Steam Elephant's* crew, wearing appropriate period attire, take a breather.

overlooked; their chain-haulage engine has been seen as a dead-end on the road toward the adhesion-worked locomotive, yet *Steam Elephant* was unknown until 2001.

Blenkinsop and Murray clearly had a strong influence on their work; *Steam Elephant* being virtually an adhesion version of a Middleton-type locomotive. While Trevithick, Hedley, Hackworth and Stephenson all had their champions, either from influential biographers or family members, Chapman and Buddle, despite being well-respected in their own lifetime, had no families who could 'fire off a broadside' on their behalf against the claims of others.[84]

Chapter 4
Billies and *Dillies* at Wylam 1814-1816

Wylam, about 10 miles west of Newcastle upon Tyne, is the birthplace of two notable early locomotive engineers: George Stephenson (1781-1848) and Timothy Hackworth (1786-1850).

The Wylam estate was owned by the Blackett family, who worked coal mines there from the 17th century. The Wylam waggonway, taking coals down to staithes at Lemington on the Tyne, was laid to five feet gauge and opened in 1748 making it one of the older waggonways in the North East. In 1800 Christopher Blackett (1751-1829) became Lord of the Manor, and in 1808 had the waggonway relaid with L-shaped cast-iron tramplates replacing earlier wooden rails. In the following year, Blackett approached Richard Trevithick to build a locomotive, but the dispirited Trevithick declined to re-enter the locomotive building field, just when a new patron might have been found. Thus, Blackett was the 'only person to show a practical interest in the locomotive between Trevithick's ... *Catch Me Who Can* of 1808, and Blenkinsop's ... engine of 1812.'[85]

BLACK BILLY AND EARLY EXPERIMENTS

The locomotive history of Wylam Colliery is shrouded in myth, claim and counter-claim from the descendants of some of those involved, such as Oswald Dodds Hedley (son of William Hedley the colliery viewer) and John Wesley Hackworth (son of Timothy Hackworth, foreman blacksmith).

William Hedley (1779-1843) was born at Newburn and was educated at Wylam. By the age of 21 he was the viewer at Walbottle Colliery, and in 1805 he was in charge of Wylam colliery. He later became interested in lead mining (1808) and then became a ship owner. In 1824 he acquired two collieries, one near Durham and one near Wylam, setting himself as a coal owner. He had four sons – Oswald, Thomas, William and George – and in 1839 established Hedley Brothers and Partners. William Hedley became a very wealthy man and died at Burnhopeside Hall in County Durham. But it was at Wylam that serious attempts were made to develop a locomotive which relied solely on adhesion rather than legs, or rack and pinion drive.

William Hedley wrote in December 1836:

In October 1812 ... I was requested ... to undertake the construction of a locomotive engine. Amongst the many obstacles to locomotion at that period ... was the idea ... than an engine would only draw after it, on a level road, a weight equal to its own. I was forcibly impressed with the idea, and which was strengthened by some preliminary experiments, that the weight of an engine was sufficient for the purpose of enabling it to draw a train of loaded waggons ... I had a carriage constructed ... placed upon the railroad and loaded with different parcels of iron ... I ascertained the proportion between the weight of the experimental carriage and the coal waggons when at the point when the wheels of the carriage would surge or turn without advancing it...[86]

This test carriage was man-powered and had a geared final drive acting on all four wheels. William Hedley in his 1836 letter implies that Trevithick and Blenkinsop did not understand that a locomotive could pull a useful load using adhesion only – despite the success of the Penydarren engine (Chapter 1).

Although trying to claim precedence in this matter over George Stephenson (1781-1848) (Chapter 5), Hedley's letter is in fact vague in terms of actual dates, and where dates have been given by later writers to fill the gap they are at best unreliable. Although there is limited evidence for the existence of the 'test carriage', Trevithick had clearly shown an adhesion-only locomotive could pull a useful load. Indeed Jim Rees has described these experiments as 'pseudo-science'.[87] The Hedleys' claim as to precedence over Stephenson (or anyone else) was challenged during the 19th century, with one reviewer noting that the locomotives of Stephenson and Hedley were contemporaries in trying to solve the same problem, but with independent points of inspiration: a claim later challenged by Hedley's family.[88] The claim over who built the first 'Locomotive engine that ever went by its own spontaneous movement along iron rails' would resurface every 10 years or so during the 19th and early 20th centuries and, as Liffen has discussed, the

ABOVE: 'Old Locomotive engine, Wylam Colliery' a water colour sketch by Thomas Hair, circa 1840. He faithfully captures the complicated valve gear and overall appearance of the engine, and unusually twin tenders. *(Beamish Museum)*

Hedley brothers were not above doctoring the past on their father's behalf.[89]

According to Nicholas Wood (1795-1865) the viewer at Killingworth Colliery (Chapter 5), the first locomotive at Wylam – *Black Billy* (Chapter 1) – was built in 1813 by Hedley and despite its irregular, jerky motion worked well enough and 'for some time ... the whole of the coals was taken taken down the Rail road by this locomotive'.

Although Robert Young in his unreliable narrative of the life of Timothy Hackworth ascribes the 'test carriage' to Hackworth alone, Wood provides a near-contemporary account describing Blackett as the originator of the adhesion trials and in having this first engine 'made' by Hedley. In fact it was Thomas Waters, engineer, of Gateshead who was engaged by Hedley to build it, and indeed Waters had succeeded John Whinfield (Chapter 1) as the local agent for Trevithick's patent high pressure engines, further strengthening the suggestion *Black Billy* was derived from Trevithick practice. Waters was paid 'on account of the Engine' between March and August 1813. Jonathan Forster, Wylam colliery enginewright, and foreman blacksmith Timothy Hackworth probably had some involvement with the three Wylam locomotives. While the role of Hackworth has been exaggerated by his family members, that of Blackett has often been overlooked.

Black Billy ended its days as a stationary engine, having 'been sold to Mr Joseph Cowen, of Blaydon Burn, to grind clay'. But even in this role it was found to be unreliable and of limited power.[90]

PUFFING BILLY, WYLAM DILLY AND LADY MARY

It is remarkable that two of the three early Wylam locomotives exist. Although known today as *Puffing Billy* and *Wylam Dilly*, they were originally named *Elizabeth* and *Jane* after Christopher Blackett's daughters. The third locomotive gained the name *Lady Mary*.[91]

Puffing Billy and *Wylam Dilly* had remarkably long working lives, being at work into the 1860s. *Puffing Billy* was loaned to the forerunner of the Science Museum in 1862 and purchased by them in 1865, while *Wylam Dilly* was purchased by two of Hedley's sons in 1869. It currently resides at the National Museum of Scotland in Edinburgh, which purchased it in 1882. *Lady Mary* was out of use by 1832.

Black Billy had shown the utility of locomotive working, but as Blenkinsop and Murray had demonstrated, a two-cylinder locomotive could dispense with a cumbersome flywheel and had a far higher power-output. The actual designer of Wylam's two-cylinder locomotives is unknown, although it's traditionally ascribed to Hedley, but there was clearly involvement from Blackett and Chapman and Buddle (Chapter 3). Chapman wrote to Buddle in May 1814:

Pray what is Mr Blackett about – I left a Plan for making his Beast act upon a chain with great simplicity compared to his complicated machine which even if it would answer would require machinery for its wheels.[92]

Thus it is likely that Chapman and Buddle had sent Blackett copies of drawings for their chain-haulage locomotive. Furthermore, Hedley's man-cranked test carriage is remarkably similar to William Chapman's rope-making machine, which also reinforces the link between Chapman, Buddle and the Wylam engines.[93] One, albeit not-contemporary, description of perhaps *Black Billy* reinforces a possible Chapman link in the use of a chain:

ABOVE: *Puffing Billy* photographed at Wylam Colliery in spring 1862; driver Joseph Pratt, fireman William Greener. *(Beamish Museum)*

ABOVE: *Wylam Dilly* photographed by R H Bleasedale at Craghead, together with William and George Hedley, in 1881. Note the misleading chalked inscription 'William Hedley 1813'. *(Beamish Museum)*

It went by a sort of cog-wheel, then there were was something of a chain to it. There was no idea that the machine would be sufficiently adhesive to the rails by the action of its own weight, but I remember a man going before – that was after the chain was abrogated – and scattering ashes on the rails in order to give adhesiveness...[94]

As noted in Chapter 1, Hedley's 1813 patent included the use of a 'rope or chain' mounted on posts down the centre of the track along which the locomotive could haul itself, analogous to Chapman's 1812 patent. As Dendy Marshall noted in 1953, there is a striking similarity between Chapman and Buddles' eight-wheel adhesion Lambton locomotive of 1814 and Hedley's two Wylam locomotives, and that Hedley and Chapman and Buddle were in fact in dispute at that crucial period.[95]

The date of these three locomotives is also contentious; although popularly described as being built in 1813 (the year of Hedley's patent), Wylam colliery accounts show that payments for boiler plates, gears, wheels, parallel motion and other components for the locomotives were made from 1814 to the middle of 1816; the final 'Balance of Account' being paid in June 1816. Furthermore, Blackett wrote to Hedley in March 1814 that the first engine was, or would soon be, at work on a trial basis.

The actual date of introduction of steam power on the Wylam waggonway is shown by the dramatic cost in the increase of repairs to the track in August 1814, rising from £5 per fortnight to as much as £47 per fortnight in January 1815 before reducing to £10 per fortnight in April 1815. As Andy Guy has argued, this sudden increase in the cost of maintaining the permanent way was most likely due to track damage by the Wylam engines, suggesting that one or both began

work in August 1814, only a month after Stephenson's *Blücher* (July 1814). Three locomotives are recorded as being in use at Wylam by January 1816. As John Crompton has noted: 'Hedley's [1836] claim that his locomotives ... had superseded the use of horses "long before" July 1814 was at best misleading, and at worst a lie'. In fact the development of the locomotive at Wylam and Killingworth was contemporaneous.[96]

BOILERS AND CYLINDERS

Puffing Billy and *Wylam Dilly* saw the re-introduction of the Trevithick return-flue boiler, putting the fire-hole and chimney at the same end of the boiler.

A return-flue boiler was more efficient than the straight-flue, providing about three times as much heating surface: 60sq ft for *Puffing Billy* compared with 20sq ft for a Killingworth locomotive. The return-flue boiler meant that more heat was transferred from the fire to the water through conduction (about 3% for a straight flue boiler and about 18% for a return flue) which also meant that there was less coal and heat wasted.[97] The boiler barrels of *Puffing Billy* and *Wylam Dilly* are both considered to date from circa 1814. *Puffing Billy*'s flue has been repaired at least once and the boiler barrel has been modified to incorporate a replacement man-hole on the boiler back plate, replacing one on the boiler barrel, the access to which was blocked by alterations to the exhaust arrangement when a cylindrical silencer was fitted, the base of which still survives. No similar modification was made to *Wylam Dilly*. *Wylam Dilly*'s boiler barrel has been extended mid-century through the addition of an extra boiler ring, the rivets of which are closed mechanically and not by hand.[98]

A more efficient boiler meant that the blast requirement to aid the through-put of

ABOVE: A full size working replica of *Puffing Billy* was built by the Deutches Museum in Munich in 1906. Every effort was made to replicate the locomotive exactly, including materials and construction methods – including all the cracks, patches and distortions of the original.

hot gases in the boiler was less than for a straight-flue boiler when pushed hard. Thus the Wylam locomotives had a relatively 'soft' blast.

Furthermore, prevention or reduction of noise was also a major requirement at Wylam with Hedley getting into a legal dispute with one of the wayleave proprietors due to the noise, and smoke, caused by his locomotives. Therefore, the exhaust steam from the two cylinders was directed into a vertical, cylindrical, silencer before being allowed to escape into the chimney, which must have considerably lessened the effect of the blast on the fire.

Hedley's sons and grandson claimed that he was the progenitor of the blast pipe, thus ignoring the crucial role of Richard Trevithick (Chapter 1) a decade earlier.

Whether Hedley was ignorant of Trevithick's work or not is unclear, but it is likely he was aware of Trevithick having had a good technical education, which makes his denial of Trevithick's achievements all the more unusual. Furthermore, given that the Wylam locomotives were still at an experimental stage in July 1814, then Hedley's claim to have introduced the blast pipe before Stephenson is also possibly spurious; the two men working independently and coming to the same conclusion that Trevithick had.

Hedley and Stephenson both had to deal with the problem of noise, leading Stephenson to soften the blast of his locomotives as much as practicable while Hedley introduced a silencer to resolve the same issue.[99]

The use of a return-flue boiler probably precluded the use of cylinders immersed

ABOVE: A fireman's-eye view of the Beamish replica of *Puffing Billy* as it raises steam, showing the firebox alongside the chimney.

ABOVE: A rear view of *Puffing Billy* showing the hemispherical end of the return-flue boiler at which the driver stood.

ABOVE: A Georgian train in a Georgian landscape: *Puffing Billy* at work on the Pockerley Waggonway, at Beamish Museum.

on the centre line of the boiler, and instead they were mounted outside close to the hemispherical end of the boiler, a design later adopted by Hackworth for his locomotives.

The cylinders used the exceptionally long stroke of 36 inches and to improve thermal efficiency they are steam-jacketed. The cylinders of *Puffing Billy* and *Wylam Dilly* are reminiscent of those used by Trevithick. The steam chest was somewhat 'squeezed up' at the top of the cylinder itself – as if they had been intended to be immersed in the boiler – and with a very long steam passage which must have been difficult to cast. As Rees and Guy have suggested, this type of cylinder is copied directly from a Trevithick-type engine, and may suggest that they were based on either a Trevithick design or re-used the pattern for the cylinder from *Black Billy*.[100]

This very long stroke made them inefficient, with only a quarter of the steam being put to useful work, and indeed the replica of *Puffing Billy* at Beamish runs very wet due to the large amount of condensation, despite the steam jacket, which takes place in the cylinder. The geared-up final drive helped overcome poor steam use.[101] Whereas Blenkinsop and Murray, Chapman and Buddle, and Stephenson used cross-heads to guide the piston rod, Hedley used the complicated 'grasshopper' motion, derived from stationary engine practice, and patented by William Freemantle in 1803, and the use of Freemantle motion was probably in response to the use of cylinders on either side of the engine. Steam was distributed using slide valves, actuated by tappets from the rocking beam of the 'grasshopper' motion.

WHEELS AND BOGIES

The three Wylam locomotives were originally delivered on four wheels. They were flangeless to run on the plateway, but as William Hedley described in 1836 – and the cost of track repairs confirm – they were too heavy for the brittle cast-iron plates.

They were almost immediately rebuilt on eight wheels, using the system of bogies patented by Chapman and Buddle in 1812. It is unlikely that the bogies were free to swivel, but they did spread the weight of the engines to prevent any further serious track damage, this work being completed by 1816. The similarities between Chapman and Buddle's bogie-mounted adhesion locomotive and the modified Hedley locomotives further reinforces the link between them. They remained in this form until 1828-1830 when they were reconstructed back to four wheels when the line was relaid with edge-rails, and *Lady Mary* was abandoned around the same time.

In 1822 *Wylam Dilly* was apparently put to work powering a paddle-wheel steam boat on the Tyne during a strike of Tyne keelmen.

While Hedley may not have made the major breakthroughs in locomotive design that he or his family claimed he did, he deserves his place in railway history.

Together with Blackett (and others) he revolutionised transport on the Wylam waggonway, and two of the three early locomotives were at work into the 1850s and

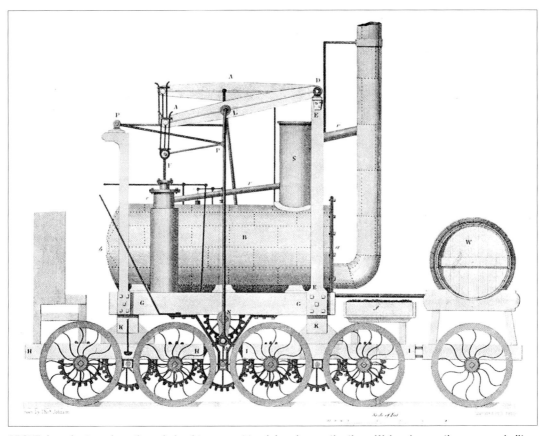

ABOVE: In order to reduce the axle load to prevent track breakages, the three Wylam locomotives were rebuilt on two four-wheel bogies.

1860s. The designs were clearly successful and indeed when, in the 1830s, Hedley was planning to introduce locomotives at one of his pits in Durham, he was happy to build another Wylam-type locomotive. Lack of further locomotive development at Wylam, however, was because the colliery had never been particularly rich (unlike Killingworth); that the three locomotives did their job satisfactorily; and perhaps that colliery management lacked sufficient vision to develop the locomotive any further. [102]

LEFT: During a Tyne keelman's strike, *Wylam Dilly* found itself converted to a steamboat, driving paddle-wheels rather than railway wheels. *(Beamish Museum)*

Chapter 5
George Stephenson
1814-1825

George Stephenson looms large in the history of early locomotives, and it is hard to deny the crucial role he played in their development.

As early as 1836 he had been dubbed the 'father of the locomotive' – which sparked heated debate ever since. Even though Stephenson did not invent the locomotive, and many of the major breakthroughs had already been made, he was an intuitive engineer who had a systems-wide approach to problems and conceived an integrated system of steam locomotives working on a specially constructed track.

He was one of the first engineers to recognise the need for development of the track as well as the locomotive – and especially its wheels – referring the wheel and rail as belonging together like 'man and wife'. He was good at taking and refining others' ideas and was a vocal advocate of the locomotive, continuing to build them when other engineers had more or less given up on locomotive development.[103]

WHY KILLINGWORTH?

While his early life has been subject to much myth-making by his biographer Samuel Smiles, Stephenson was a self-taught mechanic who excelled at his job, coming to the attention of his influential employers. George was the second of six children born to Robert Stephenson, a 'fireman' responsible for working one of the pumping engines at Wylam Colliery.

Eventually settling at Killingworth Colliery, George soon came to the attention of Ralph Dodds (circa 1763-1821), the viewer and was 'widely admired for his experience and ability'. Dodds, like Stephenson, was largely self taught, and worked hard to further his own skills, but crucially both men were supported in their engineering endeavours by their employers.

It was at Killingworth that Stephenson built up a team of engineers around him,

ABOVE: George Stephenson, the 'father of the locomotive' as he was dubbed by Dr Dionysius Lardner.

ABOVE: George Stephenson's birthplace at Wylam. The Wylam Waggonway ran right past the Stephensons' front door – no wonder George was fascinated by railways. *(Lauren Jaye Gradwell)*

some of whom would stay with him for the remainder of his career, including Nicholas Wood (1795-1865), the viewer, who had also studied under Dodds, and with whom George worked on numerous experiments on locomotives and track.[104]

While Stephenson had a genius for practical mechanics and engineering, as Robert Hartley has described, George was surrounded by other 'brilliant minds working on related problems' and, crucially, had the encouragement of his employers and thus their financing for his early locomotive projects.

He was also able to curry favour with other influential engineers and industrialists, including John Birkenshaw of the Bedlington Iron Works and William Losh (1770-1861) of Messrs Losh, Wilson and Bell of the Walker Iron Works; Stephenson was a regular Sunday visitor to the Losh family's elegant town house 'gaining access to a widening world of wealth and intellectual awareness'. This was probably thanks to the Rev William Turner (1761-1859), to whom George's only son Robert (1808-1859) had come to the attention of while studying with John Bruce at the Percy Street Dissenter's Academy. Turner was minister of Hanover Square Unitarian Chapel, Newcastle's leading place of nonconformist worship. The chapel was a hot-bed of intellectual talent, and these relationships opened many doors for the ambitious Stephenson.[105]

THE *BLÜCHER*

George's first locomotive was *Blücher*, built for the Killingworth Colliery. George had perhaps been inspired to build *Blücher* – which may have also been named *My Lord*

– thanks to the Rev William Turner who had visited Leeds during the summer of 1812 and had seen the Blenkinsop-Murray locomotives at work.

That August Turner presented a paper on steam locomotion to the influential Literary & Philosophical Society of Newcastle, which was widely reported in the press. No doubt this was in part responsible for the introduction of Blenkinsop-Murray locomotives on the Kenton and Coxlodge Railway, a few miles to the west of Newcastle, in 1813. Furthermore, the owner of Middleton Colliery, Charles Brandling, lived in Newcastle; Matthew Murray was also a Tynesider as was Blenkinsop, who took care to 'keep tabs' on developments in their home area.[106]

Work began on *Blücher* in the early part of 1814 and 'first tried' on the Killingworth Railway on July 25, 1814. It was small and lightweight (so as not to damage the track)

and embodied many of the features of the Blenkinsop-Murray machines – a geared final drive (with the same 2:1 ratio); cylinders set on the centre-line of the boiler and immersed therein; and a single flue tube boiler.

They used the same 8 x 24 inch cylinders as the Leeds originals. Unlike the Middleton engines which were of 'single fill' type, George provided a tender to carry coal and water, and (rather as Chapman and Buddle with *Steam Elephant* (Chapter 3)) had a wrought iron tank around the chimney which was heated by the exhaust gases acting as a water heater to improve efficiency.

At first steam appears to have been discharged into the atmosphere *à la* Blenkinsop and Murray, but the engine was short of steam and could go no faster than about 3mph. Therefore, in order to improve steam raising, Stephenson directed the exhaust steam into the chimney as Trevithick

ABOVE: Killingworth West Moor colliery (as it appeared in 1881), where George Stephenson came to prominence and built his first locomotives.

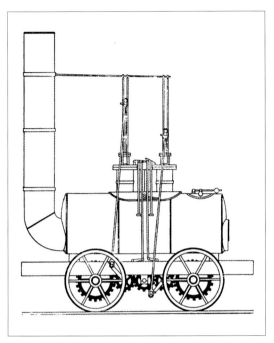

ABOVE: A tentative reconstruction of *Blücher*, probably George Stephenson's first locomotive.

had done 10 years before which 'at once doubled the power of the engine, enabling her to go six miles an hour and maintain her steam'.[107] Nicholas Wood wrote in 1825:

> *To effect a greater rapidity, or to increase the draught of the chimney, Mr. Stephenson thought that by causing the steam to escape into the chimney through a pipe with its end turned upwards, the velocity of the current would be accelerated, and such was the effect.*[108]

Peter Davidson has noted that thanks to the forced blast, *Blücher* could generate twice the amount of steam than a Middleton locomotive which didn't use that technology (or need to). Most of this steam, however, would have been wasted due to the long-stroke cylinders and the geared final drive. Despite these problems, *Blücher* was clearly fit for purpose.[109]

The use of a single, large diameter boiler flue burning often poor quality coal did not require a high degree of vacuum to be created at the chimney end to draw the fire. In fact a strong blast on such a boiler would have the effect of wasting fuel by ejecting most of it out of the chimney.

The other consideration was of course noise, which could scare horses and upset neighbouring landowners. Thus, Stephenson reduced the blast of the Killingworth locomotives as far as practicable. But, by sticking rigidly to a single flue boiler, the only way Stephenson could increase steam generation was to gradually increase the strength of the blast, but this was sacrificed in his later locomotives (e.g. *Locomotion*) through increased coal consumption, as the stronger blast ripped the fire apart, with upwards of half of the fuel being lost via the chimney.[110]

PATENT LOCOMOTIVES

Blücher had been first demonstrated in July 1814, and within a year George had not only built a second locomotive but obtained a patent too (February 28, 1815). This second locomotive was 'first tried' on March 6, 1815, only a week after he and Ralph Dodds' patent had been published. Their employers (Lord Strathmore and Mr Wortley, two of the 'Grand Allies' of North East Coal Owners) had been suitably impressed by the work of the two men, and had agreed to pay the costs for them to obtain their patent (£158 12s 4d). Perhaps as further reward, they increased Dodds' salary to £200 per year and Stephenson's to £100. Clearly Stephenson and Dodds were 'fully committed to the locomotive project' which had won the approval of their influential employers.[111]

In their joint patent, Stephenson and Dodds outlined the basis of the 'Killingworth' type locomotive – two cylinders immersed on the boiler centre line, the boiler having a single

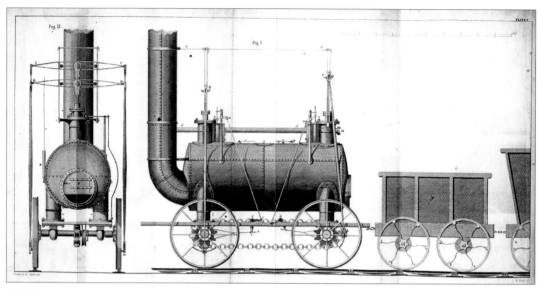

ABOVE: Stephenson and Dodds' patent locomotive of 1815, which established the basic 'Killingworth' type, shown as rebuilt with larger wheels.

flue tube. Thus far analogous to the work of Blenkinsop and Murray, but Dodds and Stephenson dispensed with the geared drive and instead drove the wheels via connecting rods. While this was a marked improvement on the geared drive, it was in effect a return to Trevithick practice: *Catch Me Who Can* used connecting rods and crank pins. In order to ensure synchronisation of the cylinders, at first a crank axle and inside coupling rods were used, but the technological limitations of the time meant that they had to be abandoned in favour of chain coupling.

The 1815 locomotive was larger and heavier than *Blücher* and was 'found to work remarkably well'. Further development of the locomotive appears to have been suspended for the remainder of the year as Stephenson worked on his safety lamp, returning to work on the locomotive and track in the following year resulting in a second patent, this time with William Losh.[112]

Unfortunately for Stephenson, his 1815 patent was probably rendered void by a locomotive 'of the same construction' which

had been run on the Newbottle waggonway before his and Dodds' patent had been published. The similarity in the locomotive designs was probably the use of chains to couple the wheels, which had first been proposed by William Chapman in 1814 and by William Tindall and John Bottomley of Scarborough, who were both associated with Chapman.

Nicholas Wood in his 1825 *Treatise*, which extolled the work of his friend Stephenson, conveniently overlooked this matter. Then there is also the question of the involvement of Chapman and Buddle in the 1815 patent, as Dr Joseph Hamel, the agent for Tsar Alexander of Russia, who had visited Newcastle and environs in November 1814, wrote to John Buddle in January 1815 seeking their consent for drawings of the engine as well as a model of it. Thus it is likely that the more experienced Chapman and Buddle gave assistance to the as-yet inexperienced Stephenson in obtaining his patent and in the design of the locomotive.[113]

Stephenson's second patent was joint with the ironmaster William Losh. He had studied metallurgy in Sweden – then considered to be producing the best iron in Europe and Scandinavia – and chemistry in Paris; in 1802 Losh established a chemical works at Walker on Tyne and an iron founders and engineers (Losh, Wilson & Bell) in 1809. Via his brother James (1763-1833), the recorder of Newcastle, he was aware of George's work with the miners' safety lamp.[114] The 1815 design was taken further with the weight of the engine being spread over six wheels and carried on 'steam springs' which utilised steam at boiler pressure as an early kind of shock absorber: sufficiently strong steel plate springs had yet to be developed which could carry the weight of a locomotive. Whilst a clever idea, the steam spring did not work on the boiler pressures of the day. The 1816 patent with Losh was not just concerned with locomotives, but the rails they ran on, and wheels as well.[115]

WHEELS AND RAILS

George recognised that in order for the locomotive to improve, it was not the locomotive alone which needed technical study, but the track and wheels, too. Thus he applied himself not only to the evolution of the locomotive but the track on which it ran, making a study of wheels (and how wheels performed) and the rails they ran on. Indeed, Andrew Dow has described:

A railway [is] a transport machine, one part of which is the movable, consisting of the rolling stock, and the other part fixed,

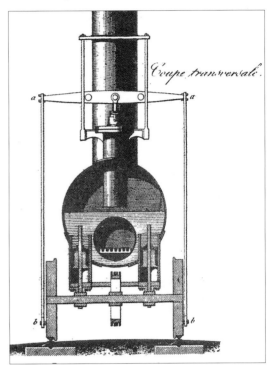

ABOVE and BELOW: Stephenson and Losh patent locomotive of 1816 which was carried on six wheels and 'steam springs' in order to mitigate track damage.

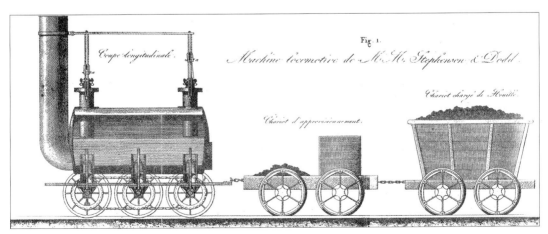

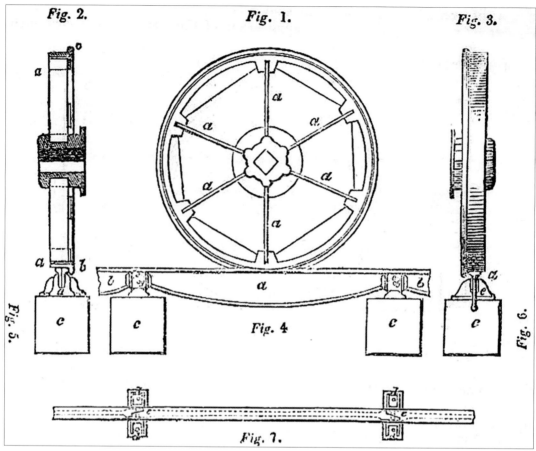

ABOVE: Stephenson and Losh's patent of 1816 also included rails and wheels; George referring to the rail and wheel as 'man and wife'.

comprising the permanent way and its auxiliaries ... The several parts are dependent upon one another, and together they constitute the railway transport machine.[116]

One of the characteristics of railway wheels is the use of a flange and a coned tread. The flange guides the wheel while the cone helps keep the wheel centred on the head of the rail. However, it is likely that early wooden locomotive wheels were not coned, which would explain why they are described as being so damaging to the permanent way.

Although Andrew Dow has suggested the coning of iron wheels to be an accident of their method of manufacture, the coach designer William Bridges Adams suggests coning

was due to George Stephenson who 'found considerable difficulty in preventing the wheels running off the rails, notwithstanding the very large flanges'. At the same time (1829-1830) in the USA, Jonathan Knight, the engineer of the Baltimore and Ohio Railroad, was experiencing the same problem and he proposed the use of coned iron wheels, first a ratio of 1:6, later 1:5.[117] The coning also helped wheels pass around curves where the inside and outside wheels would be travelling at different speeds, something also recognised by Nicholas Wood.[118]

Stephenson and Losh's patent covered both wheels and rails. They included two types of wheel: the first was cast iron with wrought iron spokes and cast iron hubs and rims. The second were cast iron with reverse S-shaped spokes. The patent rails were fish-bellied, supported on chairs and with half-lap joints which gave a far smoother ride.

Stephenson and Losh's cast iron rails were superior to others which had been in use before, but when it came to the question of rails for the Stockton and Darlington Railway despite his own financial interest in the use of cast-iron rails, George (much to the chagrin of Losh) favoured the wrought iron rails recently patented by John Birkinshaw at the Bedlington Iron Works near Morpeth. The Killingworth railway was relaid with them in 1820 and the Heaton in 1821.

Although contemporary commentators thought that wrought iron rails would de-laminate and not be as durable as cast iron, these wrought or 'malleable' iron rails proved themselves to be superior: they were stronger and not as brittle as cast iron; could be produced in longer lengths, thus reducing the number of joints; reduced the cost of repairs; but were more expensive to purchase than cast iron, however. It was with wrought iron rails that the next generation of railways such as the Liverpool and Manchester would be laid, the rail having evolved to meet the demands of the locomotive.

THE STEPHENSON LOCOMOTIVE

It was at Killingworth where George developed the 'Killingworth' type locomotive, of which he built six for Killingworth and five smaller designs for the Hetton Colliery. He also built in 1816 a locomotive for the Kilmarnock and Troon Railway, and in 1819 a locomotive for the Llansamlet Colliery in South Wales.

The Kilmarnock engine was the first in Scotland. It was a six-wheeler with chain-coupled wooden wheels, having originally cost around £750. It later found its way to the Paisley and Renfrew Railway and was sold at auction for £13 and sadly broken up for scrap in 1848.[119] The 1819 Llansamlet engine was similar to the Killingworth engines but smaller, although retaining the 9 x 24 inch cylinders and a 40psi boiler. It was capable of moving 10 tons, compared with the 30-40 tons of the larger Killingworth engines. The locomotive did not remain in use for long as in 1824 proposals were being made for it to be used to pump water in a colliery.[120]

THE KILLINGWORTH TYPE 1816-1821

At Killingworth, Stephenson had already built two trial engines, in 1814 and 1815. Between 1816 and 1821 he built a further five locomotives for Killingworth: two in 1816, two in 1818 and the fifth in 1821.

They were simple, robust four wheel locomotives with the wheels coupled by chains. They used slip-eccentrics, rather than cams or tappets, to provide motion to the valve gear, an innovation courtesy of Nicholas Wood which was crucial in the development of the locomotive. Eccentrics were mounted on the leading and trailing axle, driving the valves of their respective cylinder, which was mounted in line with the axles and wheel centres. Other important technical improvements owed to Wood are the laminated steel leaf spring, strong enough to support the weight of a locomotive (1827), and also the use of wrought iron tyres on cast iron wheels which greatly improved their durability and therefore reliability.

Boilers grew progressively larger from 8ft x 3ft 9in (1816) to 10ft 8in x 4ft 6in in 1821, which also saw a lengthening of the wheelbase from 6ft 4in to 7ft. The crank's pins used spherical ends so as to always

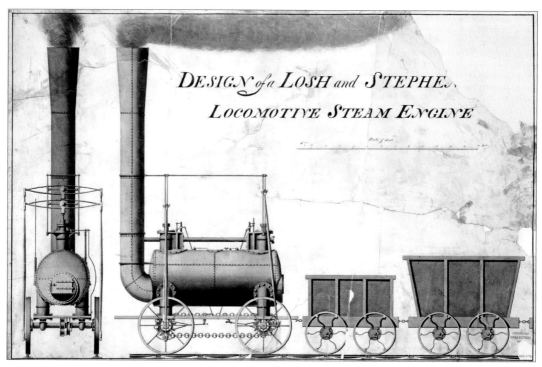

ABOVE: Simon Goodriches' drawing of a circa 1818 Killingworth locomotive probably based upon that given by Nicholas Wood, but with the chimney shown full height. *(Science & Society Picture Library)*

ABOVE: A colour-wash drawing representing an 1821 'Killingworth' locomotive. It was probably drawn by George Stephenson and was owned by him. *(Science & Society Picture Library)*

keep the coupling rods in alignment despite track irregularities. Each of these designs (1816, 1818, 1821) represented a gradual improvement in locomotive performance due to larger heating surfaces and larger wheels 'which combined to almost double the available power'.[121]

Trials with the 1821 locomotive held that June were widely reported across the North of England, and even London; the similarity of the wording of these press reports suggests the use of a pre-written 'press release', perhaps by Nicholas Wood:

Mr Geo. Stephenson made his first experiment on Monday week, at Killingworth Colliery, Durham, upon the locomotive steam engine invented by him and in the presence of a number of Gentlemen. Though the weather was unfavourable, the engine conveyed with the utmost facility (upon a railway having an elevation of one inch to the yard) of 20 laden coal-wagons, the aggregate of which, with the engine itself, may be estimated at nearly 100 tons, with an amazing degree of rapidity.[122]

ABOVE: Five locomotives of 'Killingworth' type were built for Hetton Colliery. This example proudly proclaims its builder's patent.

Benjamin Thompson (1779-1867) describes in 1822 that five locomotives were at work at Killingworth, of which 'four are kept employed' suggesting that the fifth was kept as the spare. Thus the first two trial locomotives had been laid aside by that date, and either converted to other uses or scrapped.[123]

HETTON COLLIERY

Between 1822 and 1823 George built five locomotives for Hetton Colliery. This was a line George knew intimately as in 1820 he had been responsible for the surveying and engineering of the railway to carry coal from the pits down to the Wear.

It was laid with Stephenson and Losh's patent cast iron rails. The Hetton series of locomotives were smaller and lighter than their siblings at Killingworth. The first three were built for the opening of the Hetton Railway in 1822. They had boilers 4ft diameter and 8ft long, working at 50psi. They weighed approximately eight tons and suspension was provided by Stephenson's patent 'steam springs'. They used the now standard 9in x 24in cylinders, and the wheels were 3ft 2in diameter. These three 'small'

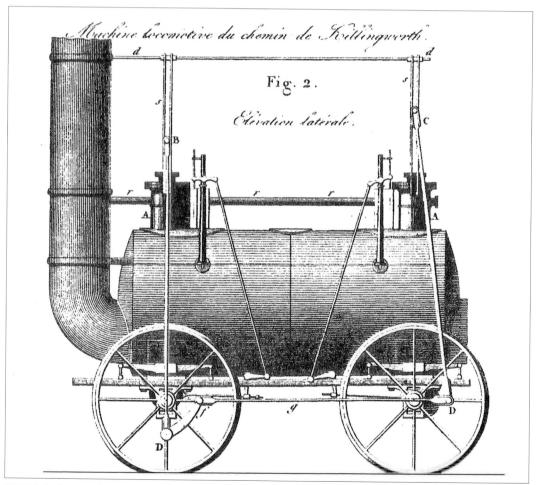

ABOVE: An improved 'Killingworth' type locomotive as depicted by Nicholas Wood. Note the use of plate springs and larger wheels, suggested by Wood.

ABOVE: Stephenson's *Billy* probably dates to 1816 and is thus the oldest standard gauge locomotive in the world. It's seen here in the 1860s at work at Hetton Colliery.

Hetton locomotives were probably named *Dart*, *Tallyho* and *Star*. Two additional locomotives were at work by December 1823. These were larger than the first three probably with boilers circa 9ft 8in long and 4ft 8in diameter. The single flue was of a larger diameter than before to help improve steam raising, and the cylinders were the same size as the smaller trio.[124]

KILLINGWORTH DEVELOPED

In 1822 Nicholas Wood carried out experiments with one of the Killingworth locomotives with 4ft diameter wheels in place of Stephenson's preferred 3ft wheels. Wood concluded that larger wheels lowered the resistance between the locomotive and the track and also led to an increase in speed. Thus Wood fitted the Killingworth locomotives with bigger wheels by 1825.[125]

Also thanks to Wood was the introduction of wrought iron tyres on cast iron wheels to improve their durability. Wood also abandoned the use of Stephenson's patent coupling chains in favour of outside coupling

rods, and replaced the unsuccessful 'steam springs' for steel leaf springs in 1827.

It was these improved locomotives which were on show in the New Year of 1825 to representatives of the Liverpool and Manchester Railway and the Birmingham and Liverpool Railway. These trials were also widely reported across the north as well as London. It was reported a 'superior' 8hp locomotive with 4ft diameter wheels was able to move a load of 48 tons 15cwt at a rate of 7-9mph up a gradient of 1 in 840. An 'inferior' locomotive (presumably with smaller wheels) was capable of moving a load of 52 tons 8cwt up an incline of 1 in 792 at 3¾ mph.[126]

KILLINGWORTH *BILLY* AND HETTON *LYON*

Previously thought to have been built for the Springwell Colliery in 1826 by Robert Stephenson & Co, *Billy* preserved at the Stephenson Railway Museum was the subject of an archaeological investigation led Dr Michael Bailey and Peter Davidson.

Billy had been presented to the people of Newcastle in 1881 as part of the Stephenson Centenary. It was placed on a plinth on the High Level Bridge over the Tyne, and it was described at the time as being 'the second locomotive made by or made under the superintendence of George Stephenson'. *Billy* had clearly been rebuilt several times, but Bailey and Davidson found that essential features such as the wheelbase and thus cylinder placement and valve gear geometry were probably unchanged, the wheelbase suggesting that *Billy* was in fact one of the two engines built for Killingworth Colliery in 1816. This makes *Billy* the world's oldest surviving standard gauge locomotive.[127]

The story of the Hetton locomotive is the reverse of *Billy*; often described as dating from 1822 it was in fact one of three locomotives built c. 1849-1854 at Hetton Colliery named *Lyon*, *Fox* and *Lady Barrington*. The latter exploded in 1858. It was built as a 'lookalike' and included many mid-19th century innovations.[128] The locomotive has recently been subject to archaeological investigation.

SELF-MADE MAN?

Long before Samuel Smiles adopted George Stephenson as his icon of the 'self-made man', he had had an excellent marketing machine in the shape of Edward Pease of Darlington, the Quaker businessman behind the Stockton and Darlington Railway. He also found an excellent ally and publicist in Nicholas Wood; Pease and Wood promoting both the machine and the man in the contemporary technical and domestic press.

Wood's seminal 1825 *Treatise on Railroads and Interior Communication* also played its part in promoting Stephenson. While it is arguably a fundamental text on early railways and locomotives, prior to publication Michael Longridge, a partner in Robert Stephenson & Co (Chapter 6), warned Pease that 'Wood's Book must undergo a strict censorship before it is published and I fear this will be a work of considerable delicacy,

ABOVE: *Billy* was presented to the Corporation of Newcastle and was placed on a plinth on the High Level Bridge in 1881 to mark the Stephenson Centenary.

ABOVE: *Billy* now resides in the Stephenson Railway Museum, just outside Newcastle. *(Robert Kitching)*

but it must be done'.

A fortnight later, Wood wrote to Edward Pease that the book would be worthwhile and necessary 'if it only be done judiciously and without injuring my friends,' in particular George Stephenson. Probably as a result of this editorial policy, Wood carefully omits his own knowledge of the possible nullification of Stephenson's Patent; fails to mention the experiments by others after 1815 or the explosion of Brunton's mechanical horse, which had done much to turn public opinion against the locomotive. Moreover, George Stephenson was becoming well-known not just as a locomotive engineer but as a *railway* engineer, not just on the home but international stage.[129]

That said, local coal owners were impressed by Stephenson; Matthias Dunn recorded in 1815 that 'George Stephenson had completely succeeded in getting 2 Travelling Engines into complete work, which save about eight horses each' and by 1819 Stephenson was a 'man of great

ABOVE: The Hetton *Lyon* locomotive was for a long time thought to date from the 1820s, but in fact probably dates from c. 1849-1854. Seen here in steam taking part in the centenary celebrations for the Stockton and Darlington Railway in 1925.

reputation and much experience in making Rail Roads'.

Edward Pease also manipulated the image of Stephenson, recommending he 'should always be a gentleman in his dress' and his speech, and that he appear smart and clean every day.[130] Stephenson was thus in a unique position: thanks to his friendship with the Peases he was able to access the friendly, entrepreneurial network of Quaker financiers; and through the Rev Turner had a connection to the socially élite and technically-minded Unitarians, whose influence far outstripped their numbers.[131]

Stephenson's success at Killingworth and Hetton, and the careful curating and marketing of his image by the Peases – astute businessmen who had clearly grasped the potential of the locomotive worked railway – resulted in a national platform for George: the Stockton and Darlington Railway, perhaps one of the most significant railways ever built.

Linking coal pits to the River Tees at Stockton via Darlington, it brought together, perhaps for the first time, many crucial concepts in the development of railways: it was a public railway, with capital held in shares; open to all users; used steam locomotives (although not exclusively) and carried passengers (albeit by sub-contractors) and goods.[132]

George Stephenson was a vocal champion of the locomotive and thanks to his pioneering work at Killingworth and Hetton, as well as the help of the Pease family, he and his locomotives came to national prominence. Stephenson was not just a locomotive engineer, but crucially a railway engineer. There is no doubt that by 1825 he was the single most experienced locomotive builder in the country.

ABOVE: *Lyon* on display at Locomotion in Shildon. *(Andrew S Mason)*

Chapter 6

Robert Stephenson & Co.
1823-1829

Robert Stephenson was George Stephenson's only son and, determined to give his boy the best start in life possible, George paid for Robert's education, including a stint at perhaps the best school in Newcastle: the Dissenter's Academy on Percy Street, run by John Bruce. There he came to the attention of the Rev William Turner (above) who took the young man under his wing. Another of Turner's pupils had been Michael Longridge of the Bedlington Iron Works.

ABOVE: Robert Stephenson who, while only in his 20s, transformed the steam locomotive.

Robert was eternally grateful to the Rev Turner for the polish he gave to his education, and it was thanks to Turner that many doors were opened, including the influential Newcastle Literary and Philosophical Society and the fledgling Newcastle Mechanics' Institute, of which George chaired the first meeting. The Rev Turner was the founding secretary and gave the inaugural address. Members included John Buddle (Chapter 3) and the Loshes (Chapter 5).[133]

Robert Stephenson & Co. was established in June 1823 as an engineers, engine builders and millwrights, and although the firm would go on to primarily build railway locomotives, of its first 49 orders, 28 were for stationary steam engines, the first of which was delivered to the Earl of Carlisle in December 1823.

The company was established thanks to the influence of the Peases of Darlington. The capital was £4000 in 10 shares divided between Edward Pease (4), George Stephenson (2), Robert Stephenson (2) and Michael Longridge (2). Although aged only 21, Robert Stephenson was the managing director to 'superintend its ... operations, to supervise the building operations and engage men, take orders, advise on contracts, draw plans, make estimates, keep the accounts, and in all matters great or small govern the ... establishment on his own responsibility.'[134]

Unfortunately for the firm, Robert and his father had a serious disagreement and

Robert, coming under the influence of the Quaker banker Thomas Richardson, was encouraged to take part in the 'Colombian Mining Association' on a salary of £500. Robert was in Colombia from July 1824 to November 1827, the silver mining venture in South America not necessarily being a success.

On the way home, he came across an impoverished Richard Trevithick (Chapter 1) who had also been lured to the silver mines of South America, and Robert paid for his ticket home. It was also at this period that George Stephenson was away from Newcastle, being involved with the Stockton and Darlington Railway and the first Liverpool and Manchester Railway Bill. This meant that there was no effective management at Forth Street, and very limited technical direction.

Robert returned to the helm in January 1828 and his drive and energy certainly revolutionised Forth Street – its locomotives

ABOVE: Nicholas Wood, the viewer at Killingworth Colliery to whom Robert was apprenticed, and who is credited with the introduction of plate springs, larger wheels and wrought iron tyres to the locomotive. *(After Dendy Marshall, 1930)*

ABOVE: Perhaps some of the most famous gates in the world; those of Robert Stephenson & Co, Forth Street, Newcastle.

ENGINE USED IN CONSTRUCTING THE LIVERPOOL & MANCHESTER RAILWAY, 1828-9.

ABOVE: Despite the spurious and obviously incorrect caption, Springwell Colliery No. 2 was built for the Springwell Colliery in 1826 and was photographed by R E Bleasedale in 1862.

reaching new heights of development, resulting in a frenetic 33 months of work which culminated with the delivery of *Planet* in October 1830.[135]

SPRINGWELL AND *LOCOMOTION*

The first two locomotives ordered from Robert Stephenson & Co were for Springwell Colliery, costing £550 each, although their delivery was delayed until 1826 by the order for *Locomotion* et al for the Stockton and Darlington.

They had the usual 9 x 24 inch vertical cylinders and incorporated many improvements over the earlier designs including, for the first time, outside coupling rods in lieu of chains, and pivoted 'cannon box' axle boxes. Whereas *Locomotion* etc used Freemantle motion, the two Springwell engines used the Killingworth system of cross-heads. They also used outside coupling rods.[136]

The final evolution of the locomotive as essayed by George Stephenson was *Locomotion* and its sister locomotives for the Stockton and Darlington Railway (S&D). Designed by George and built by Robert Stephenson & Co, *Locomotion* was an enlarged version of a Killingworth locomotive, the two major differences being the substitution of the more complicated Freemantle 'grasshopper' parallel motion in place of the simple cross-head arrangement; and the use of outside coupling rods rather than chains.

The actual overall design of *Locomotion* was worked out in the absence of both George and Robert Stephenson. That said, however, George certainly had some input into the design as there is an annotated sketch in George's own hand working out the valve gear for the S&D locomotives, which was later worked up by staff at Forth Street.

The use of Freemantle motion rather than the Killingworth arrangement was probably derived from the works' stationary engine, and was certainly a retrograde step. There are at least two 'project' drawings dating 1824-1825 showing alternative forms of valve gear, one of which is covered with George Stephenson's handwriting noting that the valve gear should be parallel motion similar to that of the Etherley stationary engine supplied by Stephenson & Co for the S&D. Both locomotives were late in delivery and 'bore marks of uncouth design and rough construction' and consequentially suffered from mechanical problems. Two more locomotives, followed in 1826 to ostensibly the same design, and a fifth in 1827.

Although known to history as *Locomotion* (Samuel Smiles incorrectly named the locomotive *Active* in his first edition, but corrected it in his second), *Hope*, *Black Diamond* and *Diligence*, Stockton and Darlington locomotives were in fact numbered rather than named, and the earliest reference to the name *Locomotion* only comes in 1833.[137]

As Brian Reed has noted, given the problems at the Forth Street works at the time, it is surprising that the four locomotives were delivered at all.

Although now fitted with cast iron 'Plug Wheels' as developed by Robert Wilson of Gateshead, it is certain *Locomotion* et al were delivered with wooden wheels. In lieu of springs, the rear axle passed through a wrought iron tube and guides, analogous to a modern cannon-box axle box to provide some rudimentary three-point suspension. While *Locomotion* had this type of suspension on the rear axle, the three later locomotives had it on both. The use of this form of suspension precluded the use of coupling chains and led to the introduction of outside coupling rods which were first used on these locomotives. It also precluded the use of two eccentrics to work the valves, so on *Locomotion* the valves for both cylinders were derived from a single slip-eccentric mounted on the fixed leading axle.[138]

Evidence from the replica locomotive shows that the fire was prone to clinkering and the boiler often short of steam; analysis

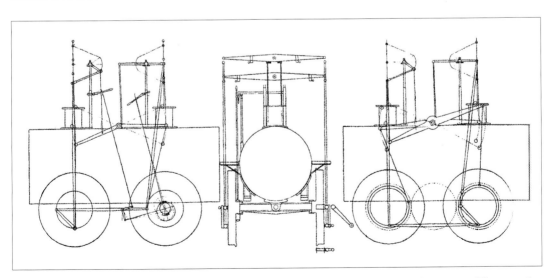

ABOVE: Working drawing for 'Locomotive Engine Darlington' trying to work out the valve gear and its geometry. Two different arrangements are shown; that on the left was adopted. *(After Warren, 1923)*

ABOVE: *Locomotion* was one of the earliest locomotives to be preserved, being put on public display in 1857. This colour postcard was posted in 1901.

ABOVE: The original *Locomotion* taking part in the Stockton and Darlington Centenary Celebrations of 1925, albeit propelled by a petrol engine in the tender.

by Peter Davidson has similarly shown that *Locomotion* had small power reserves and could be badly affected by a head-wind. That said, *Locomotion* et al were significantly more powerful than the Killingworth locomotives (11hp compared to 7.5hp) and had to be, not because the loads hauled were significantly heavier but because the distance covered was so much greater. *Locomotion* pulled the opening train on the S&D consisting of 21 coal wagons, a passenger coach carrying the directors, and about 500 passengers sat in the wagons. The 'Locomotion' type is recorded as being able to a load of 31 tons at a speed of 5mph up a gradient of 1 in 264.

In order to improve steam generation, by 1833 *Locomotion* was fitted with a main flue with two return tubes, later a main flue with a single return tube, and finally back to a single main flue, all within the original boiler shell. It was also apparently rebuilt with six wheels and springs. The material remaining from 1825 is probably the boiler barrel, cylinders and valve gear.[139] After having been mounted on a plinth at North Road Station, Darlington in 1857 and later (1895) removed to a plinth at Bank Top Station, *Locomotion* now resides at the Head of Steam Museum at the former North Road Station in Darlington.

'OLD ELBOWS'

The sixth locomotive built for the Stockton and Darlington Railway was the enigmatic *Experiment,* aka 'Old Elbows' from its peculiar construction.

ABOVE: *Locomotion* forms the centrepiece at the Head of Steam Museum, Darlington.

ABOVE: Detail of *Locomotion*'s complicated valve gear. To change direction the valves had to be set by hand.

ABOVE: The replica tender coupled to *Locomotion*, perhaps dating from 1857 when the engine was 'restored ' for public display.

The actual designer of the locomotive is unclear: Robert was still in South America and in 1826 George had moved to Liverpool to supervise the construction of the Liverpool and Manchester. From his letters, however, it appears that George had some input in the design, albeit remotely; certainly John Urpeth Rastrick (chapter 7) assigned the design to George.

Experiment was the first attempt to break away from the Killingworth arrangement and to re-introduce horizontal cylinders to the locomotive. At that time it was believed horizontal cylinders were not desirable as the weight of the piston in the cylinder bore would wear it oval. Through using horizontal cylinders, Stephenson was also able to counter the 'hammer blow' effect on the track caused by vertical cylinders. George wrote to Robert in February 1827:

My new plan of locomotive it will be a huge job the Cylinder is intirly within the Bolior and neaither Cranks nor chain will be wanted. I have no fire door and I will not use more than coals that has heather to been used you will think I have mistaken some ideas about this but I think not – and you may depend upon it that if you do not get home soon every thing will be at perfection and then there will be nothing for you to do or invent...[140]

A pair of horizontal cylinders 9 x 24 inches were immersed in the upper half of the rear of the boiler. The piston rod was guided by parallel motion and worked a very long connecting rod to a pair of wheels at the leading end. As built it was an 0-4-0 with wooden wheels 4ft diameter and coupled with outside rods. There was a single boiler flue, the firebox being at the same end as the cylinders, which would have made tending the fire somewhat difficult especially while the engine was at work. The fire grate used hollow water-filled fire bars and there was also an internal water drum.

Experiment had an 18 month gestation. Upon delivery it was found to be overweight and in March 1828 the S&D committee ordered it was to be 'laid off until it be placed on six wheels' and fitted with springs. This work was completed by October by Timothy Hackworth (1786-1850) the 'Superintendent of the Permanent and Locomotive Engines' on the S&D. As a result, Hackworth was ordered by the S&D committee to place the entire stock of S&D locomotives on six wheels and fit them with springs. It appears that Hackworth went to Killingworth (at the company's expense) to view the locomotives there 'with springs and malleable iron rims' which had been introduced by Nicholas Wood (Chapter 5).

In its rebuilt form Rastrick notes *Experiment* ran 'from Stockton to Darlington … taking up 20 empty waggons the Engine and Tender included 39 tons at the rate of 12 Miles per hour.' It was later rebuilt with vertical cylinders at the firebox end of the boiler and was apparently worn out by 1833.[141]

LANCASHIRE WITCH

Upon his return to Forth Street in January 1828, Robert Stephenson wrote to Michael Longridge:

I have been talking a great deal to my father about endeavouring to reduce the size and ugliness of our travelling engines, by applying the engine either side of the boiler, or beneath it entirely, somewhat similarly to Gurney's steam coach … Mr Jos. Pease writes my father that in their present complicated state they cannot be managed by 'fools', therefore they must undergo some alteration or amendment. It is true that the locomotive engine, or any other kind of

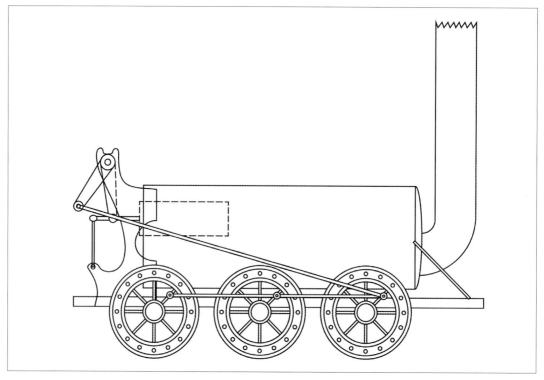

ABOVE: *Experiment* aka 'Old Elbows' was the first attempt to re-introduce horizontal cylinders after Trevithick over a decade earlier. It must have been a difficult locomotive to work, with the firebox at the same end as the cylinders. *(Andrew S Mason)*

engine may be shaken to pieces; but such accidents are in a great measure under the control of enginemen, which are, by the by, not the most manageable class of beings. They perhaps want improvement as much as the engines.[142]

Lancashire Witch was the first locomotive which incorporated Robert's design ethos to simplify locomotive construction and operation. It was also the first locomotive to be built for the Liverpool and Manchester Railway (L&M) – the world's first intercity double-track mainline railway – and the first to burn coke as the L&M Act forbade locomotives from making smoke.

The boiler of *Lancashire Witch* was designed by the technically-minded Henry Booth (1789-1869), who was secretary and treasurer of the L&M. He had first approached the board with his idea for a coke burning boiler in April 1827 and requested £100 to carry out experiments. In January 1828 a 'drawing of the boiler was exhibited' and approval was granted to build the locomotive, to be able 'to draw 20 tons of goods and fifty passengers' to weigh about six tons and cost £550. The engine was subsequently transferred to the Bolton and Leigh Railway.

Lancashire Witch was a step change from previous designs: although Robert retained long stroke cylinders (9 x 24 inches) from his father's engines, they were placed on either side of the boiler and inclined at an angle of 39° (to reduce hammer blow) with a direct drive to the leading wheels, which were coupled via outside coupling rods. The wooden wheels were 4ft in diameter and

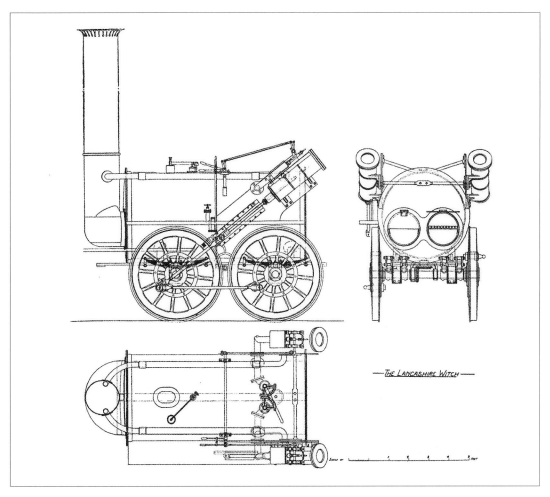

The Lancashire Witch

ABOVE: *Lancashire Witch* was built for the Liverpool and Manchester Railway. It was the first locomotive to burn coke and was the first Stephenson locomotive to use angled cylinders and to have direct drive to the wheels. *(After Warren, 1923)*

had wrought iron tyres. The use of inclined cylinders and a wrought iron bar frame meant that all four wheels could be fully sprung. The slide valves were worked by eccentrics on the leading axle and could be worked expansively, using a rotating plug valve driven from bevel gears on one of the axles. Two toothed quadrants controlled the amount of cut-off.[143]

The boiler was 9ft long and 4ft in diameter and, as first designed, had a main flue with two smaller flues running parallel to the main flue. Running through the main flue were two small diameter water tubes. The fire was urged using a forced draught supplied by bellows worked from eccentrics under the tender.

In attempting to burn coke, Henry Booth was applying existing black-smithing technology (bellows) to introduce sufficient air to the fire for the coke to burn efficiently. Stephenson wrote to Timothy Hackworth in July 1828 that 'the engine works beautifully. There is not the least noise about it. We have also tried the blast to it for burning coke and I believe it will answer'.

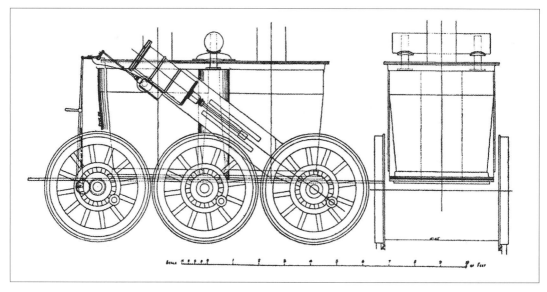

ABOVE: *Twin Sisters* no doubt earned its sobriquet from having two boilers and two chimneys. The boilers had been designed by Henry Booth to burn coke and prevent smoke. *(After Warren, 1923)*

This letter is often used by his detractors to suggest that Stephenson did not understand the blast pipe, when this is not the case. As Peter Davidson has described, Stephenson did understand the blast pipe but a major contemporary consideration was keeping noise to a minimum. The fact that Stephenson places emphasis on 'there is not the least noise' suggests that he was taking care to avoid making a loud noise which would have scared horses, and upset the influential, and often anti-railway landowners along the route.[144] The bellows were probably pretty soon given up because as Marc Séguin in France and John Braithwaite and John Ericsson at Rainhill discovered, they absorbed most of the power of the locomotive to work them.

Lancashire Witch was rebuilt with a twin straight flue boiler (uniting at the chimney end) with twin fireboxes and was a turning-point in the design of the Stephenson locomotive: it was compact; had direct drive from cylinders to the wheels; had a frame and was fully sprung; had expansive valve gear; and was easier to operate than what had gone before. Thus it would influence all subsequent designs, including the famous *Rocket* of Rainhill.

TWIN SISTERS

The second locomotive for the Liverpool and Manchester was also a coke-burner, the twin-boilered *Twin Sisters*. As with *Lancashire Witch*, the boiler was designed by Henry Booth but the form of the twin boilers is, unfortunately, unknown.

Twin Sisters, alias the 'Liverpool Coke Engine', was under construction in December 1828. In order to expedite progress building the line, in March 1829 – i.e. a month before the proposal of the Rainhill Trials – the board 'thought it desirable to work part of the line between the Marle Cutting at the West of Olive Mount and the Broad Green Embankment with a Locomotive Engine'. George Stephenson was 'directed to provide an engine for this purpose' which he reported would be ready in six to eight weeks.[145]

Uniquely it had two vertical boilers and two chimneys (no doubt hence the name), but like *Lancashire Witch* used the same 9 x 24 inch cylinders mounted at 40° driving six coupled wheels, developing about 12hp. The steam could also be worked expansively and all six wheels were sprung. Boiler pressure was 50psi. Various experiments were carried out with regards to the efficiency of the blast and position of the blast pipe, as noted by George Stephenson:

I put on to the coke engine a longer exarsting pipe, riching nearly to the top of the chimeney but find it dose not do so well as putting it in the chimeney lower down. I think it will be best near the level of the top of the boiler.[146]

The locomotive had arrived by early July and was at work by the middle of that month, where it did the work of 'about 10 horses' on construction duties, and was capable of moving the then prodigious load of 54 tons at about 8mph. The boiler was refilled with warm water, heated to 70° by boilers placed at intervals along the line. *Twin Sisters* won fulsome praise from the local press who declared her 'the best … we have ever seen'. Unlike horses which grew tired, the locomotive did not and as John Dixon reported to the L&M board, could work night and day, saving in man- and horse-power:

The cost of working for 12 hours say for coal, attendance and oil, 13s 8d, and to do the work of about 10 horses, or when working night and day the work of 20 horses for 27s 4d.[147]

With the arrival of *Rocket* in October 1829, *Twin Sisters* was put to work at the Liverpool end of the line with *Rocket* being used on the Chat Moss contract. She was still at work in February 1831 on permanent way and ballast duties when she was involved in a fatal accident at Liverpool Road Station, Manchester.

Twin Sisters was never numbered or formally taken in stock, and was broken up in December 1831, and one of the cylinders used to work a water pump at Manchester station.[148]

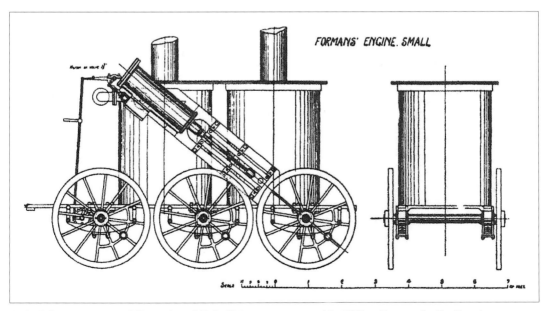

ABOVE: A narrow-gauge (3ft) version of *Twin Sisters* was proposed for William Forman for the Penydarren plateway. *(After Warren, 1923)*

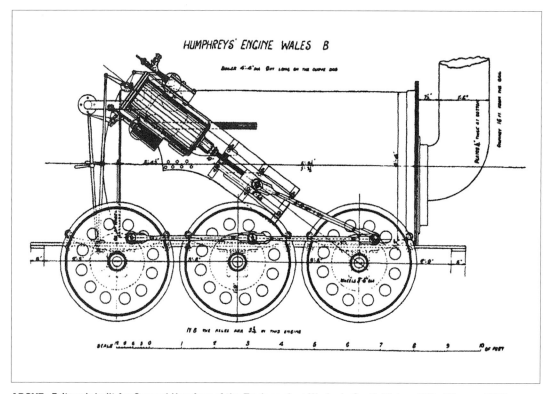

ABOVE: *Britannia* built for Samuel Homfray of the Tredegar Iron Works in South Wales. *(After Warren, 1923).*

A narrow gauge (3ft gauge) version was proposed for William Forman of the Penydarren Iron Works in South Wales, where Trevithick had built his famous locomotive (Chapter 1). It was designed to run on a plateway rather than edge rails. Although designed with twin boilers, the engine as delivered had a single, horizontal boiler (2ft 9in x 7ft 2in) containing a straight flue which was elliptical in section. The cylinders measured 7 x 20 inches and the wheels were 3ft in diameter. It was despatched together with the *Britannia* (below) from Newcastle by ship to South Wales on July 18, 1829. The engine worked successfully for two years before being returned to Newcastle in 1832 for conversion to 4ft 6in gauge when the opportunity was taken to fit it with a multi-tubular boiler utilising the original boiler barrel. An outside

sandwich frame was provided and it was converted to an 0-4-0 with new wheels (3ft 4in) and a crank axle.

In overall appearance it was similar to a contemporary Stephenson Samson class 0-4-0 luggage engine albeit with inclined outside cylinders at the firebox end.[149]

Another Stephenson locomotive supplied to South Wales was the *Britannia*, an enlarged 0-6-0 version of *Lancashire Witch* ordered by Samuel Homfray of the Tredegar Iron Works. It too was designed for a plateway.

Rather than the twin flues of the lighter, faster *Lancashire Witch*, in order to increase the heating surface in these 0-6-0 mineral engines, Robert Stephenson adopted the return-flue boiler as typified by Trevithick, Hedley and Hackworth. *Britannia* cost £550. It could generate about 8hp, and was capable of pulling a load of 53 tons at approximately 6mph.

ABOVE: Marc Séguin, the 'father' of modern French railways.

Sadly on its first run in December 1829 its lofty chimney collided with an overhanging tree, which caused the engine to come off the tramplates and caused some damage to the chimney.[150]

LOCOMOTIVES FOR FRANCE AND AMERICA

Robert Stephenson & Co began its international reputation as a locomotive builder with two locomotives for Marc Séguin (1786-1875) in March 1828, costing £550 each, for the Chemin de Fer de Saint-Etienne à Lyon. Séguin was the nephew of Joseph Montgolfier the pioneer balloonist. He is credited with the invention of the wire-cable suspension bridge.[151]

Séguin and his brothers had first experimented with steam propulsion in 1825 in the form of two steam boats intended to run a packet service on the Rhône, using engines imported from Taylor and Martineau

ABOVE: This contemporary print of the Chemin de Fer de St Etienne – Andrézieux has a distinctly Blenkinsop-looking locomotive hauling a train of equally British-looking chaldron waggons.

of London. However, these engines proved defective and the boilers short of steam and the business soon got into difficulties. But it is for his multi-tubular locomotive boiler, which pre-saged that of *Rocket,* for which he is perhaps best remembered. Séguin was engineer of the St Etienne-Lyon Railway and on his first visit to Britain in 1825 toured the Stockton and Darlington Railway. Together with several colleagues he returned between December 1827 and February 1828. During this second visit he ordered two locomotives from Robert Stephenson & Co. This pair of locomotives unusually had vertical cylinders (9 x 24 inches) mounted between the wooden, 4ft diameter, driving wheels. Dissatisfied with the steam-raising properties of the boilers of his steam boats and of the Stephenson locomotives, he carried out a series of tests on experimental multi-tubular boilers as a means of greatly increasing the heating surface. He was granted a patent for his multi-tubular boiler in February 1828. It had a battery of 47 flue tubes and a separate firebox. The idea of a multi-tubular boiler was not new, however: the Marquis Jouffroy d'Abbans (1751-1832) – the inventor of the steam boat – had designed one with 43 tubes in 1783; Charles Dallary (1754-1835) had designed but not built one in 1803, while Philippe Gengembre (1764-1838) had designed and patented a multi tubular stationary boiler in 1821.[152]

Séguin rebuilt one of the Stephenson engines with a version of his patent boiler, the artificial draught for which was provided by fans mounted on the tender. This was because the many tunnels precluded the use of a tall chimney as Stephenson used. Very quickly, however, the fans were given up in favour of a 'steam jet' in the chimney, analogous to the blast pipe, at the suggest of the physicist Pierre Pelletan. This locomotive

was under construction in May 1829 and first steamed in July. Séguin, unlike Stephenson, preferred a separate firebox as easy to build and maintain.[153]

The St Etienne-Lyon line was designed primarily to carry coal, but also carried both passengers and goods. A variety of motive power was in use. Horses were used to pull passenger trains uphill to St Etienne, but they were allowed to freewheel downhill from St Etienne under the control of a brakesman.

Goods trains used the same method of operations, while locomotives were used to haul coal trains. Like George Stephenson in Britain, Séguin was also interested in track technology. Whereas in Britain the fish-bellied form was the norm, based on his observation of the rails on the Stockton and Darlington, Séguin preferred a parallel rail – predating the adoption of parallel rail in Britain by several years – but due to technological limitations in France at the time, they were cast rather than wrought iron, produced in relatively short 60cm lengths at the famous Le Creuzot ironworks. He also carried out his own experiments on the rolling resistances of rail-borne vehicles.[154]

The first of many locomotives sent to the USA by Robert Stephenson & Co was for the Delaware and Hudson Canal Company (D&HCC), having been ordered by Horatio Allen (1802-1889).

Ultimately four locomotives were ordered by the D&HCC; one from Forth Street and three from Foster & Rastrick of Stourbridge (Chapter 7). The Stephenson locomotive, often erroneously called *America,* was named *Pride of Newcastle* and was almost a duplicate of *Lancashire Witch.* The boiler was 9ft 6in long and 4ft 1in diameter. There were twin flue tubes 1ft 7in diameter providing steam at 50psi to two inclined cylinders 9 x 24 inches. It was built to a gauge of 4ft 3in,

ABOVE: A working replica of Marc Seguin's first locomotive was first steamed in 1987 by the Association pour la Reconstitution et la Preservation du Patrimonie Industriel.

ABOVE: A depiction of a later Séguin-type locomotive with a separate firebox at the rear of the boiler and a smokebox and chimney at the opposite. Note the large steam dome, vertical cylinders and the crew apparently divided between either end of the locomotive.

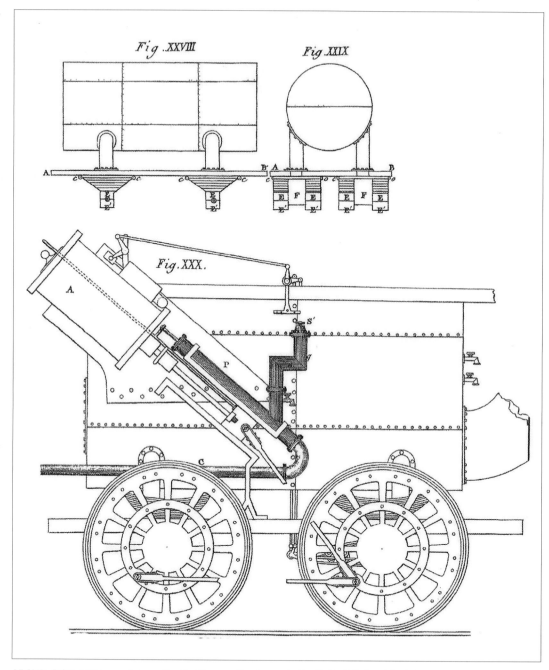

ABOVE: *Pride of Newcastle* was the first locomotive to run in the United States. The boiler and suspension arrangement are shown in the upper portion of this drawing of *Lancashire Witch*.

and the wheels were wooden, 4ft diameter at 6ft centres.

Whereas *Lancashire Witch* could be worked expansively, the 'expansion apparatus' was omitted and an 'ordinary regulator put in'. There were also differences in the frames and springing between *Pride* and *Witch*.[155] *Pride of Newcastle* arrived in New York on January

15, 1829 and was steamed on blocks, but thereafter little is known.

The imported locomotives are usually described as being too heavy for the wooden strap rails then in use in the USA, but in fact the track had been under-engineered due to limited knowledge of the weight of locomotives by engineers in the USA. The subsequent history of the locomotive is very sketchy with one unfounded rumour suggesting it exploded. A wheel and cylinder have been preserved at the Smithsonian, although at one time unwittingly were assumed to be parts from *Stourbridge Lion* (Chapter 7).[156]

The second American locomotive was ordered by Captain George Washington Whistler (1800-1849) for the Baltimore and Ohio Railroad. Like Horatio Allen, he travelled to Britain to observe best practice and met Thomas Telford, George Stephenson, Jesse Hartley and other luminaries of the early railways.

Whistler's locomotive was a six wheel version of *Lancashire Witch*, costing £560. The boiler was slightly smaller than that for *Pride of Newcastle*, 9ft long and 4ft diameter and while *Pride* used twin straight flues, Whistler's engine had a return flue, tapering from 1ft 10in at the fire end to 1ft 6in at the

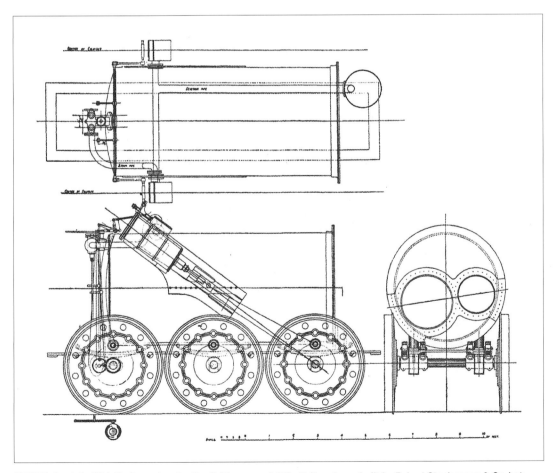

ABOVE: Captain Whistler's engine for the Baltimore and Ohio Railroad was built by Robert Stephenson & Co, but sadly lost at sea. It was probably similar to the design shown here. (After Warren 1923)

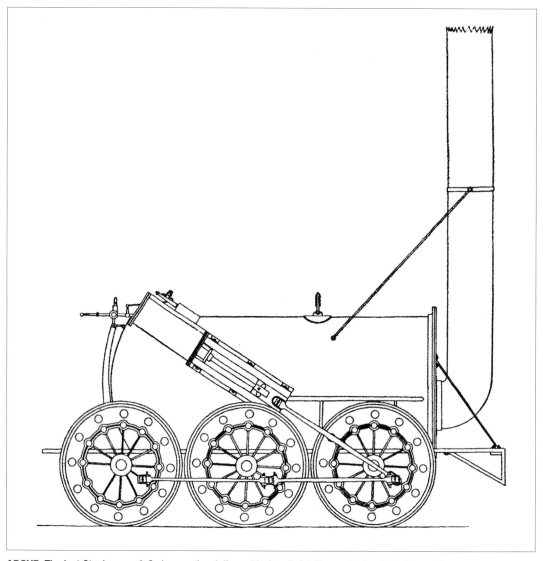

ABOVE: The last Stephenson & Co locomotive delivered before Rainhill was *Rocket*, built for the Stockton & Darlington Railway. Unlike its more famous namesake it used a return-flue boiler. *(After Warren, 1923).*

chimney end. The cylinders measured 10 x 20 inches. The wheels were iron. Sadly, Whistler's engine was lost at sea, and only the boiler was recovered.[157]

DARLINGTON *ROCKET*

The last locomotive Robert Stephenson & Co delivered before the Rainhill Trials was *Rocket* for the Stockton and Darlington in September 1829, having a return-flue boiler, inclined cylinders (10½ x 20 inches), and carried on six fully sprung wheels.

It was the first Stephenson locomotive to carry that name and cost £550. Also supplied was a spare flue tube (£26 1s 6d) and chimney (£3 2s 22d). It is ironic that the last Stephenson locomotive to be delivered before *Rocket* with its revolutionary multi-tubular boiler had a return-flue boiler of Hedley and Hackworth soon to be rendered obsolete. Yet, as Dr Michael Bailey has noted, if *Rocket*'s multi-tubular boiler had not been a success, it is likely it would have been despatched to Rainhill with a return-flue boiler. *Rocket* was sold out of service in 1841.[158]

Although outside the scope of this book, in just 33 months, Robert Stephenson not only turned-around the fortunes of his namesake firm, but transformed the lumbering colliery locomotives of his father. Via *Lancashire Witch*, and *Rocket*, he produced locomotives capable of working trains to the new requirements of a fast, regular timetabled service on the Liverpool and Manchester Railway, which would soon be joined by the other early mainline railways. Finally, *Planet,* delivered in October 1830, was the culmination of this period of intense activity by Robert and his team at Forth Street and was the first truly 'modern' locomotive.

Chapter 7

Going in a different direction – Hackworth and Rastrick 1824-1829

George and Robert Stephenson were influential in directing the trajectory of the evolution of the steam locomotive, and indeed Robert and his team at Forth Street were to do much to develop the locomotive from the (albeit refined) colliery locomotive to a machine capable of working a timetabled railway service.

ABOVE: Timothy Hackworth, the dour locomotive superintendent of the Stockton and Darlington Railway.

Not all locomotive builders followed the same path, and for their own reasons stuck to more tried and tested ideas forgoing – as George Stephenson put it – 'the danger of too much ingenuity'. Working contemporaneously with Robert Stephenson were Timothy Hackworth of Shildon and John Urpeth Rastrick of Stourbridge, who broke the mould being quickly established by the Newcastle concern.

TIMOTHY HACKWORTH

We've already met Timothy Hackworth. He was born in the same pit village of Wylam as George Stephenson. He was the son of John Hackworth (died 1804), the foreman smith who had held that position for 20 years. Timothy was educated in the village and apprenticed at Wylam colliery as a smith, and in 1807 was appointed foreman smith in his father's stead aged just 21.

While present at Wylam he would have witnessed Hedley's three locomotives (Chapter 4), and his grandson Robert Young claims he was ultimately (although unlikely) responsible for the design. Young also tries to claim, based on selective reading of Trevithick's 1802 patent, that the Cornishman did not adopt the blast pipe, or if he did had

ABOVE: 'Soho Cottage', Shildon, where the Hackworths set up their family home.

not understood it, and furthermore did not appreciate locomotives could be worked by adhesion alone, thus ascribing those key developments to his grandfather, Hackworth.

The dates presented by Young for the development of the three Wylam locomotives cannot be supported by recent research. Given that Timothy Hackworth resigned from his post at Wylam over Sunday working in 1815 there is a possibility he had left Wylam before *Puffing Billy*, *Wylam Dilly* and *Lady Mary* had been completed and commenced work. That said, however, he was undoubtedly present at Wylam when the test carriage and *Black Billy* were being constructed.[159]

In 1816 Timothy was foreman smith at Walbottle Colliery, and worked there until 1824. At both Wylam and Walbottle he gained considerable experience with colliery winding and pumping engines.

Due to the prolonged absence of George and Robert Stephenson from Newcastle, Hackworth was taken on at Robert Stephenson & Co. Hackworth was 'an experienced engine wright with the practical skills necessary to supervise component manufacture and engine erection'. Hackworth left Forth Street in late 1824, and was recommended by Stephenson to the position of 'Superintendent of the Permanent and Locomotive Engines' on the Stockton and Darlington Railway in May 1825, on a salary of £150 (rising to £200 by 1832) 'the company to find a house, and pay for his house, rent, and fire'. He would resign this position in 1840.

During this period Hackworth probably prepared a design for an 0-4-0 locomotive for South Wales. It had a straight-flue boiler, vertical cylinders on each side of the boiler, a water heater around the base of the chimney, and used outside coupling rods.[160] Hackworth was an able, practical engineer, and his day-to-day tasks for the S&D were not limited solely to stationary engine and locomotive work, and he was involved in supervising a wide array of general engineering work on the S&D. He was also responsible for establishing the first locomotive and engineering facilities for the S&D at New Shildon.[161]

CHITTAPRAT

Robert Wilson (1781-?) of Gateshead had witnessed the Gateshead Trevithick locomotive of 1805. He was a whitesmith and steam engine builder, with premises on Forth Street, Newcastle. Wilson was friends with Robert Stephenson senior (1788-1837), a younger brother of George Stephenson (Chapter 5), and from their correspondence it appears that his first (and only) locomotive, *Chittaprat* was under construction 1824-1825, with Wilson informing Stephenson in January 1825: 'I have this day set my men

to paint and finish of the Travler & I mean to clead it in so as to make it look as well as passable'. This suggests that the boiler was clad with timber and the iron work painted to protect it from rust.

Stephenson, who was then working under John Urpeth Rastrick on the Stratford and Moreton Railway, was obviously interested in the locomotive, especially as Wilson was short of funds – he had probably invested all his working capital in it. Indeed Wilson has been described as an 'ingenious self-taught … engineer and engine maker'. Wilson notes: 'You are talking about sending for the Traveler, I am glad of it I wish you had her and I had the money an article I am very much in want of at Present'. Eventually he sold *Chittaprat* to the Stockton and Darlington.[162]

Technical details of the locomotive, as well as sketches of it, were made by Marc Séguin

ABOVE: The remains of Hackworth's Soho Works at Shildon, now part of Locomotion museum.

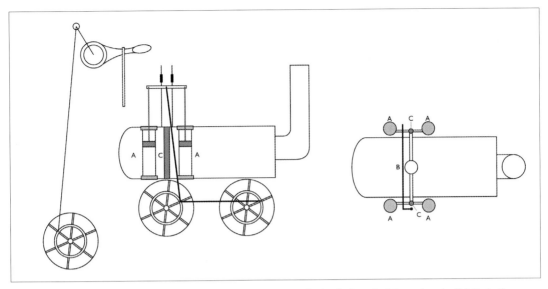

ABOVE: Re-drawn from Marc Séguin's sketch of *Chittaprat*. A vertical cylinders; C piston valves to distribute the steam. *(Andrew S. Mason)*

(Chapter 6) during his visit to Britain in 1825. It was a small four-wheel locomotive with a return-flue boiler and mounted on cast-iron 'plug wheels', a design later developed by Robert Stephenson & Co, and by Hackworth to whom his grandson erroneously ascribed the design.

These wheels were cast as an inner and outer part: the inner part was turned true on a lathe and the outer secured using wooden plugs. The boiler was 10ft 10in long and 4ft 4in diameter, and was later re-used by Hackworth, albeit lengthened, for *Royal George*. The flue tapered from 26 inches at the fire end to 18½ at the chimney end. Unusually *Chittaprat* had four cylinders. The cylinders (6 x 20 inches) were vertical, working upwards via cross heads which yoked the piston rods together, working long connecting rods, driving via cranks set at 90°. Thus, there were two cylinders on each side of the engine, grouped in pairs. The iron wheels were 47 inches in diameter and coupled with outside rods. Steam was distributed using piston rather than slide valves, driven by eccentrics on a horizontal shaft passing across the top of the boiler, coupled to the crank pins on the wheels.[163]

ROYAL GEORGE

For all its technological innovations, *Chittaprat* does not appear to have been a success. At the same time that Wilson was struggling with *Chittaprat*, the Stephenson locomotives on the Stockton and Darlington were not living up to expectation; the S&D management committee expressed 'its dissatisfaction' and 'disappointment' toward the locomotives from Forth Street. Their poor build quality, and poor steam-raising ability resulted in Hackworth approaching his employers for permission to build his own locomotive.

The major problem with *Locomotion* and its sisters was poor steam raising. So, in order to improve the ability to make steam, Hackworth returned to the return-flue of Trevithick and Hedley. He re-used the boiler of *Chittaprat*, which he lengthened to 13 feet; he probably also re-used the return flue. By so doing he increased the heating surface to 120sq ft, twice that of the 60sq ft of *Locomotion* and six times that of Stephenson's 1816 Killingworth locomotive (20sq ft). The boiler had a working pressure of 50psi and had two safety valves, a 'dead weight' valve set to 48psi and a spring-loaded valve set to 52psi. The spring-loaded safety valve was not new, owing its origin to Matthew Murray who used them on the series of locomotives he built 1812-1815 (Chapter 2). Rather than using a coil spring as Murray had done, Hackworth used a stack of 12 elliptical plate springs.[164]

In comparison with one of Stephenson's locomotives, *Royal George*'s more efficient boiler meant that there was less heat wastage

at the chimney and from unburned coal. It also meant that the boiler required only a relatively soft blast, especially compared with contemporary Stephenson locomotives which had a relatively strong blast. The use of a return flue meant that while the area of boiler in direct contact with the fire remained the same as with a straight flue, there was a greater surface area exposed to conducted heat, so that the hot gasses could do more useful work in heating the water.[165]

Secondly, having thus been able to generate more steam, Hackworth used it more efficiently than Stephenson by using more compact cylinders (11 x 20 inches). This, combined with direct drive from the cylinders to the large wheels recommended

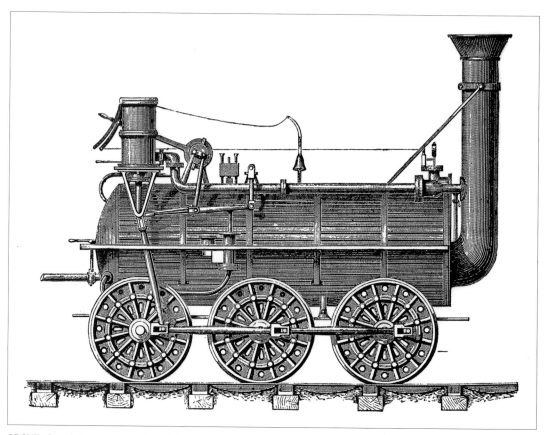

ABOVE: *Royal George* was Hackworth's first locomotive, re-using the boiler barrel (albeit lengthened) and probably the cylinders and four of the wheels of *Chittaprat*. *(Beamish Museum)*

by Nicholas Wood (Chapter 5), meant that Hackworth managed to more than double the useful power output.

These (compact cylinders; direct drive) were two crucial developments in locomotive technology.[166] Just as Robert Stephenson had set his design parameters to simplify the locomotive, so too Hackworth. Instead of the cumbersome Freemantle motion of *Locomotion* et al, Hackworth inverted the cylinders (so that they drove downwards), the piston rod acting directly on a crank-pin on the wheel. A major leap forward in locomotive design but one which is often overlooked in the 'Battle of the Blastpipe' which detracts from Hackworth's real achievements.

The piston rods were guided by parallel motion, which also supplied movement to the eccentrics (mounted on a horizontal shaft laying across the boiler as Wilson had done) as well as the water pump. Vertical cylinders were preferred because it was then believed that the weight of the piston would cause uneven wear in a cylinder, wearing them oval. But this meant that the only way to have effective springing and suspension would be to have a large 'swept area' in the cylinders to accommodate the additional movement of the crank pins. Furthermore, it also restricted the springing of driven axles, as most of the thrust of the piston would be absorbed by the springs. Whereas Robert Stephenson would adopt inclined cylinders as a halfway house as a means of springing powered and un-powered axles, Hackworth stubbornly retained vertical cylinders in his locomotive designs into the 1840s, although latterly driving to a jack-shaft so that all wheels could be sprung.

Whilst it is certain *Royal George* was carried on a wrought-iron frame, it is likely that it was not sprung until after October 1828 when the S&D ordered all its locomotives to

mounted on springs. Two visiting Prussian engineers referred to the first and second axles being 'carried by levers so that the wheels can adjust themselves to the unevenness of the road'. Thus the long leaf springs acted as both suspension and a compensating beams. The rear, driven, axle was fixed. Indeed a brass model of *Royal George*, probably by Hackworth himself, shares this feature. By January 1829 John Rastrick shows that the first and second axles were sprung, using inverted leaf-springs carried between those axles.[167]

Exhaust steam from the cylinders was passed through a feed-water heater (just as Trevithick, Stephenson, and Chapman had done) before being discharged into the chimney, the orifice of the blast pipe being coned to reduce its surface area to slightly less than that of the steam ports. Much ink has been spilled – and continues to be spilled – claiming Hackworth as the sole progenitor of the blast pipe, whilst the idea of restricting

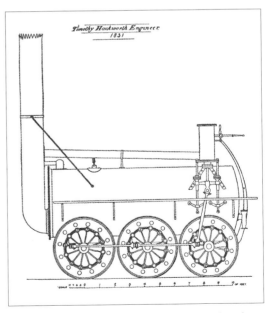

ABOVE: *Victory* was a larger, more refined version of *Royal George* using slide bars to guide the cross-head rather that parallel motion. *(After Warren, 1923)*

the orifice may have been new, the use of a blast pipe can be traced back to Trevithick in 1804.[168]

VICTORY

Royal George was 'first tried' in September 1827 and was then the most powerful locomotive on the S&D, being able to generate around 16hp, compared with *Locomotion's* 11.6hp. The success of *Royal George* inspired Hackworth to build a second, similar locomotive in 1829 named *Victory*. This was a slightly smaller (the boiler was 12ft 6in long) more refined design: the piston rod was guided by a cross-head and slide bars and the eccentrics were mounted on the rear (driven) axle with the long, curved, eccentric rods passing around the hemispherical end of the boiler. The boiler for *Victory* had been ordered by Hackworth from Robert

Stephenson & Co in September 1828, together with a spare tube, chimney and six cast iron wheels with wrought iron tyres.[169]

Hackworth was a capable locomotive superintendent, and intuitive engineer. Based upon his practical day-to-day experience of operating and maintaining the early locomotives on the S&D, he was a great synthesiser of others' ideas (return-flue boiler; spring-loaded safety valve; water-heater; blast pipe; 'plug' wheels). His major and often overlooked contribution to locomotive development was the adoption of more compact cylinders and direct drive to large wheels, which greatly increased the efficiency of the locomotive.

Hackworth went on to build a series of six-wheel mineral locomotives for the Stockton and Darlington which, whilst somewhat

ABOVE: *Wilberforce*, built in 1831, was a 'classic' example of the Hackworth-type locomotive: vertical cylinders (albeit driving through a jackshaft), a return-flue boiler and 'plug' wheels built into the 1840s.

idiosyncratic, were ideally suited to that line. He was a champion of the locomotive, and Robert Stephenson sought his counsel and operational data to refute claims that locomotives could not climb hills.

It is perhaps disingenuous to compare Robert Stephenson and Hackworth based on what happened at Rainhill: both were working in similar, and indeed overlapping fields, but while Robert was looking to develop the locomotive generally, and to make it as useful for the widest audience possible, Hackworth's engines evolved to suit a highly specialised niche, and were perhaps a dead-end outside of the working conditions of the S&D and other colliery lines in the North East.

JOHN RASTRICK

Also going in his own direction was John Urpeth Rastrick (1780-1856) of Stourbridge.

Preserved in the National Railway Museum, York is *The Agenoria*.[170] It was built by Rastrick in 1829 for the Shutt End Colliery, and compared with the replica of *Rocket,* which stands close by, looks curiously old-fashioned given both were built in the same year.

Rastrick was the son of another John Rastrick 'engineer, millwright, pump and patent churn maker' of Morpeth. He was apprenticed to his father as a millwright until the age of 15 and then went to the Ketley Ironworks in Shropshire. Around 1808 he formed a partnership with John Hazledine (1760-1810) of Bridgnorth and had the rights to produce Trevithick high-pressure stationary engines. They also built Trevithick's *Catch Me Who Can.* Hazledine died in 1810 (he has an iron tombstone) but Rastrick continued the business until 1817. Two years later, Rastrick formed a new partnership with James Foster (1786-1853) of Stourbridge.

THE AGENORIA, 1829.

ABOVE: *The Agenoria,* built in the same year as *Rocket* for the Rainhill Trials as she appeared following restoration at the Shutt End Ironworks for public display in the 1880.

Together with James Walker of London, Rastrick carried out a fact-finding mission for the Liverpool and Manchester Railway and was one of the judges at the Rainhill Trials.

Foster, Rastrick & Co. apparently built only four locomotives: *The Agenoria* for the Shutt End Colliery and three for the United States, including *Stourbridge Lion.* The four locomotives were ostensibly similar – the boiler was 10ft long and 4ft in diameter and contained a bifurcated flue tube reminiscent of *Lancashire Witch,* but with only a single firehole. The cylinders were placed either side of the boiler, similar to *Puffing Billy* and also used Freemantle 'grasshopper' motion.

Like Hedley, Rastrick also used very long stroke cylinders (8¾ x 36 inches). The chimney is perhaps the tallest locomotive chimney ever supplied, the top being 22 feet above rail level. Learning from Nicholas Wood, *The Agenoria* has 4ft diameter coupled wheels, and unusually has an early form of mechanical lubrication for the axle boxes. The present wooden frame is a later replacement. Exhaust steam from the cylinders is fed through a feed-water heater

ABOVE: The immense, giraffe-like, length of *The Agenoria*'s chimney is shown in this postcard issued by the LNER Museum at York.

before being discharged into the chimney.[171] *The Agenoria* worked the opening train of the Shutt End railway on June 2, 1829:

The locomotive, named the "Agenoria" was then attached to eight carriages, carrying 360 passengers, the weight being:

The eight carriages	*8t*	*8cwt*
Loco-motive engine,	*11t*	
tender, and water		
360 passengers,	*22t*	*10cwt*
estimated at	*41t*	*18cwt*

and the whole proceeded, attended by a band of music ... a distance of 2¾ miles, in half an hour, or at the rate of 7½ miles per hour ... On the return of the engine and passengers, carriages laden with coal to the number of twelve ... were attached to the engine, with eight carriages of passengers, the weight being ... 131 tons. The engine started with this load ... at a rate of nearly 3½ miles per hour ... The number of persons present to witness the first exhibition of a loco-motive engine in this part of the country was immense.[172]

George Stephenson, Henry Booth, and Charles Tayleur of the Liverpool and Manchester Railway visited the Shutt End Colliery Railway to observe *The Agenoria* at work: 'The engine moved smoothly from 9 to 12 miles per hour with about 20 tons of coal in 6 waggons. The Engine made very little puffing noise so common in Locomotive Engines.' They were very impressed by the use of a gauge glass for measuring the amount of water in the boiler.[173]

The Agenoria was at work until the early 1860s; certainly she was out of work in 1863 'drawn aside into a field as useless'. In 1880 she was noted 'broken down, and partially covered with grass and rubbish' by E B Marten of Stourbridge, which piqued the interest of the then Patent Office Museum, which acquired the engine in 1884. By this date the 'grasshopper' motion was 'taken off and scattered about', and one of the cylinders had been removed to work as a mine pumping engine. *The Agenoria* was restored at Shutt End Ironworks and went on display at Wolverhampton in June 1884, before being put on display at the Patent Office Museum in December, having free passage to London courtesy of the LNWR.[174]

Three locomotives were ordered by the Delaware and Hudson Canal Co in 1828 by Horatio Allen (Chapter 7). The first to arrive was *Stourbridge Lion*, which supposedly had a fierce lion's face painted on the boiler end. The first run was on August 8, 1829, with Allen at the controls. *Lion* made several successful trips along the wooden rails – made from unseasoned hemlock with a half inch thick wrought-iron strip of iron along the top:

The road had been built in the summer, the structure was of hemlock timber ... the timber had cracked and warped, from exposure to the sun ... the impression was very general that the iron monster would either break down the road or that it would leave the track at the curve and plunge into the creek ... [Placing] my hand on the throttle handle ... I started with a very considerable velocity, passed the curve in safety, and was soon out of hearing of the large assemblage present. At the end of two or three miles, I reverse the valves and returned with out accident.[175]

Trials with *Lion* continued sporadically during August and September 1829, and like *Pride of Newcastle* (Chapter 7) her later history is somewhat obscure.

Sadly the track was too lightweight for the engine, Jervis and Allen grossly underestimating the weight of the locomotives. These four locomotives represented a dead loss of $12,000 but despite this set-back the directors, in order to

ABOVE: A century of progress: *The Agenoria* on display at the National Railway Museum along streamlined giants *Duchess of Hamilton* and *Mallard. (Ian Hardman)*

get the railway running as quickly as possible therefore generating revenue, did so with horse traction. *Stourbridge Lion* was laid up until 1834 and the locomotive dispersed, with the boiler being used to provide steam for a foundry.

Between 1883 and 1901 the surviving parts of the engine – boiler, two 'walking beams' and the right hand cylinder – were collected together and displayed at the Smithsonian. A full size replica was built by the Delaware and Hudson Rail Road in 1933.[176]

FROM PENYDARREN TO RAINHILL

In the quarter century between Penydarren and Rainhill, the steam locomotive had developed from a lumbering curiosity to a machine which had revolutionised the transport of coal (and other materials) on the various colliery lines of the North East and elsewhere.

Less than a decade after Trevithick's pioneering run in South Wales, steam locomotives were used commercially at first in Leeds (1812) and then elsewhere in the industrial North by the time of the Battle of Waterloo (1815). First designed as a cheaper alternative to the horse, the steam locomotive evolved rapidly thereafter, being the motive power of the first wave of steam-powered public railways (Stockton and Darlington, Liverpool and Manchester).

While Trevithick had shown that a steam locomotive was possible, it had been the Leeds team of Blenkinsop and Murray who demonstrated that steam locomotives could be a commercial success, and their design of locomotives would go on to influence many of the later engineers working in the same field.

The evolution of the locomotive was not straight-line, with several dead ends including the use of legs or chain haulage and, once twin problems of weight and adhesion had been overcome, then so too the rack and pinion of Blenkinsop and Murray.

George Stephenson certainly stands large in this story, as he approached the twin, linked, problems of weight and adhesion as an integrated whole, recognising that the locomotive as well as its wheels and the rails it ran on were just as important as the

ABOVE: A footplate view showing the large diameter of the single boiler flue; polished brass test cocks for checking the water level; Salter-type safety valve; and the long-stroke cylinders. *(Ian Hardman)*

ABOVE: Detail of the balance weight on *The Agenoria's* driving wheel: her name clearly included the definite article. *(Ian Hardman)*

machine itself. As we have seen, building a locomotive sufficiently light so that it did not damage early rails was a major consideration, both in the UK and the USA: the failure of early imported British locomotives due to the track system being under-engineered. Both parts of the 'transportation machine' being inter-dependant and having to develop in parallel to make the whole work.

As we have seen, Stephenson was not working alone either at Killingworth or in the field of locomotive and track development.

Perhaps the fastest pace of development took place with the return of Robert Stephenson from South America. Robert, with an eye toward the fast, timetabled

ABOVE: James Renwick's 1830 drawing of *Stourbridge Lion*; the fish-bellied iron rail was erroneous as wooden rails were used. The boiler, one cylinder and two motion beams have been preserved and are on display at the Baltimore and Ohio Railway Museum.

ABOVE: A full-size working replica of *Stourbridge Lion* was built in 1933 by the Delaware and Hudson Rail Road, based on surviving original parts and *The Agenoria*. It is now on display at Wayne County Historical Society's Museum, just a stone's throw from where it ran in August 1829.

passenger service of the L&M and the lines which would follow, set out his design aims of making locomotives less ugly, simplifying construction and making them more easily operated and managed. In this he succeeded admirably in creating via *Rocket* and her sisters, and later *Planet*, a go-anywhere locomotive type suited to a variety of tasks. Other locomotive builders such as Rastrick or Hackworth, however, built their own successful machines albeit for a more specialised, local, niche in which they worked well: the 'Hackworth' type locomotive being constructed for service in the North East well into the 1840s, with *Derwent* by Kitchen & Co being built in 1845 a more refined version of Hackworth's return-flue boiler engine with twin tenders and 'plug' wheels.

Notes

1   J. R. New, 'Why displace the horse?' ER6, pp.58-70; A. L. Dawson, 'The British Mounted Arm and the Domestic Horse Trade 1814-1818' via https://www.napoleon-series.org/military/organization/Britain/Cavalry/Miscellaneous/DisposingofHorses.pdf

2   'Markets &c' Cumberland Paquet (21 December 1824), p. 3;'Newcastle Fair', *Cumberland Paquet* (1 November 1825), p. 3; 'All Hallow Fair', *Manchester Mercury* (15 November 1825), p. 4; 'Markets', *Newcastle Courant* (15 March 1828), p. 3; 'Hints to Farmers', *Waterford Chronicle* (12 April 1828), p. 4 notes 'good draught horses' fetched 'extraordinary' prices.

3   J. Rees & A. Guy, 'Richard Trevithick & Pioneer Locomotives', ER3 pp.191-220.

4   Rees & Guy, 'Trevithick', pp. 193-194.

5   M. R. Bailey, *Locomotion. The world's oldest steam locomotives* (Stroud: The History Press, 2014), p.18.

6   Rees & Guy, 'Trevithick', pp.203-204.

7   Guy et al, 'Penydarren re-examined' ER6, pp. 150-151 and pp. 182-186ff.

8   Ibid, pp. 188-189.

9   Ibid, pp. 149-159. See also Bailey, *Locomotion,* p. 19.

10   Guy et al, 'Penydarren', table 1; Rees & Guy, 'Trevithick', p. 195.

11   Guy et al, 'Penydarren', pp. 159-161.

12   E. L. Ahrons, *The British Steam Locomotive from 1825-1925* (London: Ian Allen, 1966), p.6.

13   Rees & Guy, 'Trevithick', p. 194.

14   C.F. Dendy Marshall, *A History of Railway Locomotives down to the end of the year 1831* (London: Locomotive Publishing Co., 1953), pp. 80-81.

15   H. W. Dickinson & A. Titley, *Richard Trevithick: The Engineer and the Man,* (reprint Cambridge: Cambridge University Press, 2011), pp. 64-65ff.

16   Ibid.

17   Guy et al, 'Penydarren', pp. 166-174, and appendix 1.

18   Ibid, p. 169.

19   Guy, 'Pioneers', p. 119; Rees & Guy, 'Trevithick', pp. 195-197.

20   Dendy Marshall, *A History*, p. 21

21   A. Guy, 'Early Railways: Some Curiosities and Conundrums' ER2, p.67.

22   J. Liffen, 'William Rowley, Engine-Maker' RCHS Early Railways Group, Occasional Paper 250, p. 6.

23   J. Liffen, 'Was Hazledine & Co's High-pressure engine and boiler No. 14 part of Trevithick's Catch Me Who Can?' RCHS Early Railways Group, Occasional Paper 237, *passim.*

24   J. Liffen, 'Searching for Trevithick's London Railway of 1808', ER4, pp. 1-15

25   *The Times* (8 July 1808).

26   Liffen, 'London Railway', pp. 5-6.

27   *Lancaster Gazette* (1 October 1808), p. 3.

28   Liffen, 'London Railway', pp, 16-29.

29   Rees & Guy, 'Trevithick' pp.201-202.

30   Ibid.

31   Guy, 'Pioneers', pp. 119-120; Rees & Guy, 'Trevithick', pp.205-214.

32   'Mr John Blenkinsop', *Lancaster Gazette* (15 June 1811), p. 3; S. Bye, A History of the Middleton Railway (Leeds:

Middleton Railway Trust, 2004), 8th edition, p.17; S Bye, 'John Blenkinsop and the Patent Steam Carriages', ER3, pp. 135-136; J. Rees, *pers comm.*

33 P. M. Thompson, *Matthew Murray and the firm of Fenton, Murray & Co.* (Privately Printed, 2015), passim, but pp. 92-121 for the feud with Watt.

34 Thompson, *Matthew Murray*, pp.150-151, 208-209.

35 A. Rees, *Cyclopœdia*, (London: Longman, Hurst, Rees, Orme & Brown, 1819), vol. 34, NP, entry 'Steam Engine.'

36 E. A. Forward, 'Links in the History of the Locomotive', *The Engineer* (29 April 1910), p. 432.

37 E. Galloway & L. Hebert, *History and Progress of the Steam Engine* (London: Thomas Kelly, 1830), pp.149-152.

38 'Mr Blenkinsop's Steam Carriages', *The Monthly Magazine*, (1 June 1814), pp. 394-395.

39 M. R. Bailey, 'Blücher and after' ER6, pp. 80-81; P. Davidson, 'Early Locomotive Performance', ER6, pp. 124-142.

40 Forward, 'Links', p. 433.

41 North of England Institute of Mining & Mechanical Engineers (NEIMME) Wat 3/13/116, Watson Papers, Murray to Watson, 17 April 1813.

42 Forward, 'Links', pp. 432-433.

43 NEIMME Wat 3/13/116, Watson Papers, Murray to Watson, 17 April 1813.

44 NEIMME, Wat/3/13/107 Watson Papers, Blenkinsop to Watson, 2 August 1812.

45 'On Locomotive Engines', *The Repertory of Arts and Manufactures* (1818), p. 19; NEIMME Wat3/13/115, Watson Papers, Blenkinsop to Watson, 5 April 1813; Bye, 'John Blenkinsop', pp. 141-142.

46 A. Guy, 'Just add boiling water – the elusive railway kettle, 1804-1825' ER4, p. 303, pp. 309-310, p. 312.

47 Bye, *Middleton Railway*, p. 21.

48 NEIMME, Wat/3/112/16, Watson Papers, Blenkinsop to Watson 4 October 1813.

49 Bye, *Middleton Railway*, p. 20

50 'On Locomotive Engines', pp. 19-20; NEIMME Wat 3/112/6 Blenkinsop to Watson, 12 November 1812.

51 NEIMME, Wat/3/13, Watson Papers, Blenkinsop to Watson, 2 August 1812.

52 Bye, 'John Blenkinsop', p. 141; Bye, *pers comm.*

53 'Fifty Guineas Reward', *Leeds Intelligencer* (18 January 1813), p. 1.

54 Murray to Watson, 17 April 1813.

55 'Ingenious and highly interesting experiment', *Morning Chronicle* (7 September 1813), p. 3.

56 Guy, 'Pioneers', pp. 122-123.

57 R. S. Roper, 'Robert Stephenson, Senior, 1788-1837', ER2, pp. 26-27.

58 D. Anderson, *The Orrell Coalfield, Lancashire 1740-1850* (Stoke-on-Trent: Moorland Publishing, 1975), pp. 111-117; Bye, *Middleton*, p. 23; Dendy Marshall, *A History*, pp. 49-50.

59 Bye, *Middleton*, p. 142; Dr M. J. T. Lewis, *Steam on the Sirhowy Tramroad and its neighbours (RCHS 2020), pp. 53-54.*

60 Bye, *Middleton*, p 142; M. Clark, 'The first steam locomotives on the European mainland', ER1, pp. 224-231.

61 D. Hopkin, 'William Brunton's Walking Engine and the Crich Rail-Road' ER5, pp. 229-230.

62 'Patents lately Enrolled: Mr William Brunton's of Butterley Iron Works ...' *The Monthly Magazine* (1 February 1814), pp. 62-64.

63 D. H. Porter, *The life and times of Sir Goldsworth Gurney. Gentleman Scientist and Inventor, 1793-1875* (London: Associated University Press, 1998), p. 76.

Notes continued

64 'Two Patents … to be sold' *Stamford Mercury* (27 May 1814), p.4. Meade had patented several forms of rotary steam engine in 1808 and 1813. He went bankrupt in 1814, and his various patents and entire stock in trade of steam engines and tools was sold at auction.

65 Hopkin, 'William Brunton', pp. 234-236.

66 Ibid, p. 236. See also A. Dyer, 'The walking mechanism of William Brunton's Mechanical Travller' R&CHS Early Railways Group, Occasional Paper 231, passim.

67 Guy, 'Pioneers', p. 128.

68 'On Monday se'nnight', *The Globe* (11 August 1815), p. 4; 'Colliery Accidents', *Liverpool Mercury* (18 August 1815), p. 6. The actual number of dead is unknown, and was often exaggerated in the press.

69 Ibid.

70 For example, 'Steam Engines', *The Suffolk Chronicle* (12 April 1817), p. 2.

71 'Another dreadful accident', *Lancaster Gazette* (17 June 1815), p. 3.

72 Hopkin, 'William Brunton', p. 237.

73 Guy, 'Pioneers', pp. 132-133.

74 Dendy Marshall, *A History*, Chapter V; Guy, 'Pioneers', pp.123-125.

75 Guy, 'Pioneers', p. 134.

76 'On Wednesday week', *Tyne Mercury* (3 January 1815), p. 4; see also *Lancaster Gazette* (31 December 1814), p. 3.

77 S. Rowson and A. Guy, 'Benjamin Hall's tramroads and the promotion of Chapman's locomotive patent', R&CHS Early Railways Group, Occasional Paper 251, passim.

78 P. Mulholland, 'The First Locomotive in Whitehaven', *Industrial Railway Record*, No. 75 (February 1975), pp.177-179; J. Rees, 'The Strange Story of Steam Elephant', ER1, pp. 155-156.

79 Ibid.

80 Guy, 'Pioneers', pp. 134-135.

81 Ibid, p.133; J. Rees, 'Steam Elephant', pp.160-161.

82 Rees, 'Steam Elephant', pp. 145-152.

83 Ibid, pp. 153-155.

84 Ibid, p. 166.

85 Guy, 'Pioneers', pp. 119-120.

86 'To the Editor', *Newcastle Journal* (24 December 1836), p. 2.

87 Guy, 'Pioneers', pp. 120-121; J. Crompton, 'The Hedley Mysteries', ER2, pp.149-152; Dendy Marshall, *A History*, Chapter VI; Rees, *pers. comm.*

88 'William Hedley and the Invention of Railway Locomotion', *Yorkshire Post & Leeds Intelligencer* (5 July 1882), p. 3; 'To the editor of the Yorkshire Post', *Yorkshire Post & Leeds Intelligencer* (7 July 1882), p. 6.

89 For example 'The First Locomotive Engine', *Newcastle Journal* (20 July 1844),p. 3; 'Who invented the locomotive engine?' *Newcastle Daily Chronicle* (27 January 1859), p. 3; 'The Hedley Family', *Newcastle Courant* (28 July 1882), p. 8; 'William Hedley and Locomotive Invention', *Newcastle Journal* (24 December 1915), p.3; Liffen, 'Iconography', pp. 71-75.

90 Crompton, 'Mysteries', pp. 152-153; Rees & Guy, 'Trevithick', pp. 209-210; Guy, 'Curiosities', pp. 65-66.

91 Guy, 'Curiosities', p. 65.

92 Guy, 'Pioneers', p. 121; Crompton, 'Mysteries', p. 152.

93   Guy, 'Curiosities', p. 65.

94   Dendy Marshall, *A History*, p. 91.

95   Ibid, Chapter VI.

96   Guy, 'Pioneers', p. 121; Crompton, 'Mysteries', pp.152-153, p. 161.

97   Davidson, 'Performance', Fig 5, p. 20ff.

98   Crompton, 'Mysteries', pp. 155-161.

99   Davidson, 'Performance', pp. 136-140; Dendy Marshall, *A History*, pp. 89-90.

100 J. Rees & A. Guy, 'Richard Trevithick & Pioneer Locomotives', ER3, pp. 208-209.

101 Davidson, 'Performance', p.128 and p.134.

102 Dendy Marshall, A History, pp. 85-89; Guy, 'Pioneers', pp.121-122; Crompton, 'Mysteries', p. 153ff; Guy, pers. comm.

103 M. R. Bailey, 'George Stephenson Locomotive Advocate', *Transactions of the Newcomen Society* 52 (1980) pp. 171-179; M. R. Bailey, 'Blücher and After: A re-assessment of George Stephenson's First Locomotives', ER6, pp. 79-80. See also M. C. Duffy, 'Technomorphology and the Stephenson Traction System', TNS 54 (1982), pp. 55-74.

104 R. F. Hartley, 'Why Killingworth?' ER6, pp. 33-40; L. T. C. Rolt, *George and Robert Stephenson. The Railway Revolution* (London: Penguin Books, 1978), p. 5ff.

105 Hartley, 'Why Killingworth?', pp. 31-36; Harbottle, *The Reverend William Turner. Dissent and Reform in Georgian Newcastle Upon Tyne* (Newcastle: the Literary and Philosophical Society of Newcastle Upon Tyne, 1997), p. 118. John Buddle and the Loshes were Unitarians and attended Hanover Square Chapel during Turner's ministry.

106 A. Guy, 'North-Eastern Locomotive Pioneers 1805-1827: A re-assessment', ER, p. 123.

107 Bailey, 'Blücher', pp. 80-83.

108 N. Wood, *Practical Treatise on Railroads and Interior Communication* (London: Knight & Lacey, 1825), first edition, p. 293.

109 Davidson, 'Performance', pp. 126-136.

110 Ibid; Davidson, 'Performance', pp.136-143.

111 Hartley, 'Killingworth', pp. 32-33.

112 Bailey, 'Blücher', pp. 83-85.

113 Durham County Record Office, NCB1/JB/619, Joseph Hamel to John Buddle 2 January 1815; Guy, 'Pioneers', pp. 136-139.

114 Hartley, 'Why Killingworth', p. 34.

115 Guy, 'Pioneers', pp.129-131; Rees, 'Stephenson', pp. 183-186; Bailey 'Blücher', pp. 86-87; Lewis, 'A new locomotive drawing from the 1820s' *RCHS Journal* No. 235 (July 2019), pp.482-483.

116 A. Dow, *The Railway. British Track Since 1804* (Barnsley: Pen & Sword Transport, 2014), p. viii.

117 Dow, *The Railway*, pp. 51-52; W. B. Adams, English Pleasure Carriages (London: Charles Knight & Co, 1837) p.296ff; *American Railroad Journal*, vol. 1 no. 4 (21 January 1837), p. 52.

118 Wood, *Practical Treatise*, 3rd edition, pp.163-164.

119 Bailey, 'Blücher', p. 88; 'Sale of Locomotive Engines and Paisley', *Manchester Courier* (30 December 1848), p. 3.

120 P. Reynolds, 'George Stephenson's 1819 Llansamlet Locomotive', ER2 pp.165-175.

121 J. Rees, 'The Stephenson Standard Locomotive 1814-1825' ER2, pp. 177-200; Bailey, 'Blücher', pp. 89-98; Davidson,

Notes continued

'Performance', pp. 135-142; J G H Warren, *A Century of Locomotive Building by Robert Stephenson & Co., 1823-1923* (Newcastle Andrew Reid & Co., 1923), pp. 145-146, citing Coste & Perdonnet (1829).

122 'Mr Geo. Stephenson', *Cumberland Paquet and Whitehaven Advertiser* (11 June 1821), p. 2. See also *Lancaster Gazette* (16 June 1821), p. 3; *Hereford Journal* (20 June 1821), p. 4; *Public Ledger and Daily Advertiser* (27 June 1821), p. 2.

123 Bailey, 'Blücher', p.92.

124 Ibid, pp. 94-95.

125 E. A. Forward, 'The Stephenson Locomotives at Springwell Colliery, 1826' TNS 23 (1942), pp. 117-127; Bailey, 'Blücher', p. 97; M. R. Bailey, 'Robert Stephenson & Co., 1823-1829' TNS 50 (1978), p. 126.

126 'Rail-Roads – Locomotive Steam Engines', *Durham Chronicle* (29 January 1825), p. 4; 'Railways', *Evening Mail* (9 February 1825), p. 2.

127 Dr M. R. Bailey, lecture 'Learning through Archaeology: Killingworth Billy', 21 July 2018, Stephenson Railway Museum; Bailey, 'Blücher', pp. 98-101.

128 Rees, 'Stephenson Standard', pp. 193-195.

129 Guy, 'Pioneers', p.138.

130 Guy, 'Pioneers', p. 128 and pp. 130-132.

131 M. C. Jacob, *The First Knowledge Economy* (Cambridge: Cambridge University Press, 2014), p. 47ff; R. Watts, *Gender, Power and the Unitarians in England 1760-1860* (London: Routledge, 2013), pp. 99-101ff.

132 Guy, 'Pioneers', pp. 130-131.

133 Harbottle, *William Turner*, p. 50, p. 104, and pp. 118-119ff.

134 Warren, *A Century*, pp. 53-59.

135 Ibid, pp.61-72; Bailey, 'Robert Stephenson', pp. 123-127; B. Longridge, *Rocket Man with Cousin Jacks. Robert Stephenson in Columbia 1824-1827* (Robert Stephenson Trust, 2016), passim.

136 Forward, 'Springwell Colliery', *passim*.

137 T. R. Pearce, *Locomotives of the Stockton & Darlington Railway* (HMRS, 1996), pp. 29-31; B. Reed, *Loco Profile 25: Locomotion* (Windsor: Profile Publications Ltd., 1972), passim, but pp. 19-20 for names.

138 Reed, *Locomotion, passim*; Pearce, *Locomotives*, pp. 28-34.

139 Reed, *Locomotion, passim*; Satow et al, *Locomotion, passim*; Davidson, 'Performance', pp.127-143.

140 W. O. Skeat, *George Stephenson. The Engineer & his letters* (London: Institution of Mechanical Engineers, 1973), pp. 103-104. Original spelling retained.

141 Warren, *A Century*, pp. 121-125; Pearce, *Locomotives*, pp. 47-52.

142 Warren, *A century*, p. 143.

143 Ibid, Chapter IX.

144 Ibid; Davidson, 'Performance', pp.136-143.

145 The National Archives (TNA), London: RAIL 371/1, Liverpool & Manchester Railway, Directors' Meeting, Minutes 16 March 1829.

146 Warren, *A Century*, p. 156.

147 TNA, RAIL 371/1 Directors' Meeting, Minutes 17 August 1829.

148 TNA, RAIL 371/1 Directors' Meeting, Minutes 6 July 1829, 13 July 1829; 'The New Loco-Motive Carriage', *Chester Chronicle* (31 July 1829), p. 3; 'Progress on the Railway', *Manchester Mercury* (25 August 1829), p. 2; 'Melancholy Accident', Liverpool Mercury (11 February 1831), p. 6; Dendy Marshall, *A History*, pp. 141-142.

149 M. J. T. Lewis, 'Steam on the Penydarren. Part 2: Locomotives' *Industrial Railway Record*, No. 59 (April 1975), pp. 12-32.

150 National Railway Museum (NRM), York: ROB/2/4/1 Robert Stephenson & Co., Description Book 1831, p. 3; Dendy Marshall, *A History*, pp. 142-144; Lewis, *Sirhowy*, 62-63.

151 R. de Prandières, *Souvenirs de la vie privée de Marc Seguin* (Lyon: Rey, 1926), passim.

152 Dendy Marshall, *A History*, pp. 135-138; C. C. Gillespie, *The Montgolfier Brothers and the Invention of Aviation 1783-1784* (Princeton: Princeton University Press, 1983), pp.168-175;F. Archard & L. Seguin, 'Marc Seguin and the Invention of the Tubular Boiler' TNS 7 (1921), pp.97-116; 'L'inventeur de la chaudière tubulaire', L'Amis des Sciences (25 Février 1855),pp. 60-61.

153 Archard & Seguin, 'Marc Seguin', pp.107-109.

154 M. Seguin, *Mémoire sur la Chemin de Fer de St. Etienne à Lyon* (Paris: Didot, 1826), *passim*; M. Seguin, *De l'influence des Chemins de Fer* (Paris: Carillian-Goeury et Dalmont, 1839), *passim*; *Lois Européenes et Americaines sur les chemins de fer* (Saint-Étienne: Gonin, 1837)pp.167-170.

155 NRM. ROB/2/4/1 Robert Stephenson & Co., Description Book 1831, p. 2; L. Coste & A. A. Perdonnet, 'Machine Locomotives', *Annales des Mines*, Vol. VI (1829), p. 199-202 and pp.288-289; Dendy Marshall, *A History*, pp. 140-141.

156 W. L. Withuhn, 'Abandoning the Stourbridge Lion', ER3, pp.156-164; J. H. White, *American Locomotives: An Engineering History, 1830-1880* (Baltimore: John Hopkins Press, 1968), pp. 240-241.

157 NRM, ROB/24/1 Robert Stephenson & Co., Description Book 1831, pp. 3-4; Dendy Marshall, *A History*, pp. 145-146.

158 Bailey, 'Robert Stephenson', pp. 126-127; Pearce, *Locomotives*, p. 52-54.

159 R. Young, *Timothy Hackworth and the Locomotive* (Lewes: The Book Guild, 2000), Third edition, pp.49-50ff; Dendy Marshall, *A History*, pp. 171-172; Crompton, 'Mysteries', p. 152.

160 Bailey, 'Robert Stephenson', pp. 112-113; Lewis, 'New locomotive', pp. 476-486.

161 D. Hopkin, 'Timothy Hackworth and the Soho Works, c.1830-1850', ER4 pp.280-281; Dendy Marshall, *A History*, pp.171-172.

162 Roper, 'Stephenson Senior', pp.29-30 and p. 34.

163 Dendy Marshall, *A History*, Chapter XII; Pearce, *Locomotives*, pp. 35-38; Forward, ' Springwell Colliery', pp. 119-122.

164 Pearce, *Locomotives*, pp. 46-47.

165 Davidson, 'Performance', pp.132-135 and p. 139, fig. 8.

166 Ibid.

167 Dendy Marshall, *A History*, pp. 172-174; Ahrons, *Locomotive*, pp. 5-6.

168 Ahrons, *Locomotive*, pp. 6-8.

169 Pearce, *Locomotives*, p. 54.

170 The locomotive's nameplate includes the definitive article *The Agenoria*. Agenoria is the Roman goddess of activity.

171 Bailey, *Locomotion*, chapter 4.

172 'Locomotive Engine', *Chester Courant* (16 June 1829), p. 4.

173 TNA, RAIL 371/1 Directors' Meeting, Minutes 7 September 1829.

174 J. Liffen, 'The Beginnings of Railway Locomotive Preservation', ER2, pp. 213-216.

175 Withuhn, 'Stourbridge Lion', ER3 pp. 160-161.

176 Ibid, pp. 163-164; Bailey, *Locomotion*, pp. 43-44.

Index

SELECT BIBLIOGRAPHY AND FURTHER READING

The series of international Early Railway conferences organised by the Railway & Canal Historical Society, Newcomen Society *et al*, present some of the newest research into early railways; the first conference was held in 1998 and the seventh is to be held in Swansea in 2021. The resulting papers are published by subscription only, but copies can be found at the NRM library, through the organisers, or second-hand. *Transactions*, now *The Journal* of the Newcomen Society, is also useful to the student of early railways, and the complete archive is available online to members. The *Journal of the Railway & Canal Historical Society* and the series of occasional papers published by the Early Railways Group of the R&CHS are also highly recommended.

A. Guy & J. Rees, ed., *Early Railways* (The Newcomen Society, 2001).

M. J. T. Lewis, ed., *Early Railways 2* (The Newcomen Society, 2003).

M. R. Bailey, ed., *Early Railways 3* (Six Martlets, 2006).

G. Boyes, ed., *Early Railways 4* (Six Martlets, 2010).

D. Gwyn, ed., *Early Railways 5* (Six Martlets, 2013).

A. Coulls, ed., *Early Railways 6* (Six Martlets, 2019).

The most accessible sources on early railway locomotives include the following, but some of them, such as Dendy Marshall and Ahrons, are now showing their age in terms of research, and Michael Bailey's *Locomotion* is a worthy successor:

E. L. Ahrons, *The British Steam Locomotive 1825-1925* (London: Locomotive Publishing Co. 1927).

M. R. Bailey, ed., *Robert Stephenson – The Eminent Engineer* (London: Routledge, 2017).

M. R. Bailey, *Locomotion: The world's oldest steam locomotives* (Stroud: The History Press, 2014).

M. J. T. Lewis, *Steam on the Sirhowy Tramroad and its neighbours* (RCHS 2020).

C. F. Dendy Marshall, *A History of Railway Locomotives down to the end of the year 1831* (London: Locomotive Publishing Co., 1953).

T. R. Pearce, *Locomotives of the Stockton & Darlington Railway* (HMRS, 1996).

J. G. H. Warren, *A Century of Locomotive Building by Robert Stephenson & Co., 1823-1923* (Newcastle: Andrew Reid, 1923).

The NOSTALGIA Collection

Past and Present

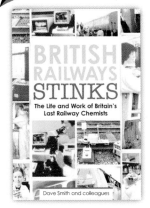

ISBN: **978-1-911658-26-9**

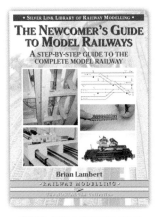

ISBN: **978-1-857943-29-0**

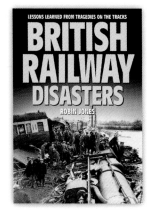

ISBN: **978-1-911658-01-6**

ISBN: **978-1-857945-58-4**

ISBN: **978-1-857945-46-1**

ISBN: **978-1-911658-02-3**

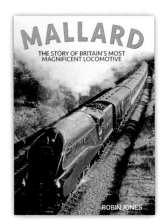

ISBN: **978-1-911658-21-4**

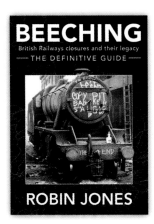

ISBN: **978-1-911658-14-6**

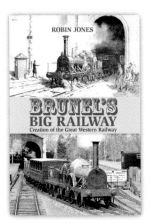

ISBN: **978-1-911658-19-1**